STEPPING OUT OF PLATO'S CAVE

Loyev Books

STEPPING OUT OF PLATO'S CAVE

Philosophical Practice and Self-Transformation

Second Edition

by

Ran Lahav

Loyev Books
Hardwick, Vermont, USA
PhiloPractice.org/web/loyev-book

ISBN-10: 0-9981330-3-5

ISBN-13: 978-0-9981330-3-4

Loyev Books

1165 Hopkins Hill Rd., Hardwick, Vermont, USA

PhiloPractice.org/web/loyev-books

Table of Contents

Loyev Books

Foreword

This book is the fruit of more than two decades of work with individuals and groups in the field of philosophical practice. Philosophical practice is an international movement of philosophers who believe that philosophy can make a meaningful difference to our lives. Philosophy, after all, means philo-sophia—love of wisdom, and it deals with fundamental life-issues which we all encounter almost daily.

I joined the philosophical practice movement in its early stages, in the early 1990s, and I soon realized that the movement was still being born, still trying to understand what it was doing. I decided to devote myself to helping to develop this new field. Thus started my philosophical journey which turned out to be at times exhilarating and at times frustrating, but always deep and rewarding. Throughout this journey I have been inspired by the vision that philosophy can deepen and enrich our lives, but at first I found it difficult to translate this vision into practice. Mainstream philosophy seemed too remote from everyday life, and too abstract and general to be of relevance to our personal concerns. It took me years of experimentation to discover, step by step, ways to address this challenge.

The approach which I am presenting here consists of several different layers and elements I have developed through the years. Earlier versions of some these elements have been published in my articles, on my website (www.PhiloPractice.org), and in a book published in Italian: Oltre la filosofia. Alla ricerca della saggezza *(Milano: Apogeo, 2010).*

I am not presenting my approach as a final doctrine. I hope that it would sow seeds for further exploration and inspire other philosophers. Philosophy, just like life, is a

*never-ending journey in a terrain that is never fully charted
and that must be discovered personally and creatively.*

Ran Lahav
Vermont, USA
www.PhiloPractice.org

Chapter 1

The Call to Go Beyond Ourselves

In his famous book *The Republic*, Plato describes a group of people sitting in a cave, tied to their chairs and unable to move. Facing the cave wall, they can see only the shadows cast by a fire burning behind them. Since they have never seen anything but shadows, they take them to be the real world.

At this point, one of the listeners remarks: "This is a strange picture and strange people." The narrator replies: "They are like us." They are like us, Plato explains, because we too are enclosed in a limited understanding of the world, and we too assume that this is what reality is like. We do not realize that it is but a mere play of shadows on a wall and that a greater and fuller reality extends beyond our cave.

One prisoner, however, is released from his bonds. At first, he refuses to look back—the light from the fire hurts his eyes, and the bright sight blinds him and confuses him. But after his eyes adjust to the light, and after he is pulled out towards the exit of the cave, little by little he comes to know and appreciate the brighter, truer world.

This is, for Plato, the role of philosophers: to step out of the cave. But their role does not end here. Their task is to go back into the cave and help release others from their shackles and show them the way out of the cave. The mission of philosophy is to make us realize that our normal world is superficial and limited, and to help us transcend our narrow boundaries and reach out towards a greater reality.

Plato's allegory of the cave touches us because it reminds us of our heart's yearning to expand our lives and live more deeply and fully. Our everyday world is usually limited to a "cave"—a superficial, comfortable routine. We go through our daily activity as if we were on automatic pilot. It is only in special moments of self-reflection that we realize how constricted our daily moments are, and then we feel the yearning to break away from these prison walls and live a bigger, richer, freer life.

Plato was not the only philosopher who wrote about this yearning. It is discussed, as we will soon see, throughout the history of Western philosophy in the writings of thinkers from virtually all historical periods and major schools of thought. This yearning expresses itself in the human heart. It speaks in the writings of great philosophers as well as mediocre ones, occasionally even in the casual conversation of the person in the street, although it is often stifled and suppressed to silence its challenging message. Because it is not easy to forsake our comfortable cave and change our familiar, automatic, and secure way of life.

This yearning speaks in many diverse languages. Different philosophers articulate it through different concepts and terminologies and metaphors, and yet they all express the same realization: that the horizons of life are broader than we commonly realize. They call us to embark upon the same endeavor: an inner transformation that would open us to greater dimensions of existence.

The details differ greatly: What is it that constricts our existence? What are the ways out of this prison? What should we expect to find outside? These questions are answered differently by different thinkers. And yet, beyond these differences they all express the same basic yearning, the same realization, the same basic call.

It is not surprising that this yearning has such diverse manifestations. Naturally, in different social settings it finds different ways of expressing itself: In ancient Greece it expressed itself through Greek concepts and values; in nineteenth-century Europe it was heard in Nietzsche's German sentences and in Kierkegaard's Danish, and in terms of the concerns and predilections of their time; nowadays it speaks in our contemporary scientific and technological metaphors. Furthermore, it articulates itself in accordance with the personality and sensitivities of the individual thinker. After all, it speaks to us through the individual's mind and heart.

I believe that virtually every reflective person knows this yearning, although in everyday life we are usually too busy to appreciate it. We are normally preoccupied with our salaries and shopping, with pleasing the boss, playing the social game, coveting a new car; and then we spend whatever little time is left in texting or watching TV. But occasionally, in special moments of self-reflection, we can hear that yearning inside us asking, "Is this all there is to my life? Shouldn't there be something more? Can't my life be richer, bigger, deeper than it actually is?"

Clara cannot fall asleep. She is lying in bed, frenzied thoughts running through her mind. At first, she tells herself that she is worried about the project she is working on—she is in charge of designing a new professional brochure for an important client. Her boss told her that it is part of an important job, and she is eager to succeed. But then she realizes that her worries are not really about her success at work. She is too experienced to worry about it. For the past fifteen years, she reflects, since the beginning of her work as a designer, she has been tackling one challenge after another. Time and again she immersed herself full-heartedly in the project assigned to her, worked frantically, stayed in her office until late at night, and finally finished it successfully only to be given the next project, and then the next project, and the next...

"How long am I going to do this?" she finds herself wondering. "Is this what the rest of my life is going to look like? My job is great, I can't complain. I am good at what I

am doing. And yet... twenty or thirty more years of this kind of work, then retirement, and then... that's it?"

She recalls her adolescence, when life seemed to promise an endless range of opportunities, when the horizons of possibilities seemed open, and the world seemed to invite her to do anything she wanted—anything... Now, in contrast, she feels herself to be very different, more mature, more experienced, successful and established, and yet enclosed in a narrow track: the same routine ways of doing her work, the same patterns of thinking, communicating, behaving, even feeling. *"I have become stuck in... in..."*

She ponders, trying to come up with an appropriate metaphor. A vague memory of Plato's Allegory of the Cave comes to her mind—it was mentioned in a magazine article she read a few days ago.

She turns on the light and switches on her computer. A quick Internet search brings her to Plato's text, and she reads it carefully. The allegory resonates in her deeply, but one point strikes her powerfully: that the prisoners themselves don't know that they are imprisoned. They don't even suspect that there is more to life than the shadows on the cave walls.

She pauses to think. *"Am I a prisoner of my routine? There certainly is more to life than designing brochures. But what is this 'more'? And what can I do about it—find a new job? But that would only take me from one cave to another. No, it's not a matter of changing jobs, but of changing something else, much bigger—perhaps even changing myself."*

A sense of urgency grips her. She feels a yearning to change her way of living as soon as possible, she has no idea how. Something within her seems to be calling her to wake up from her routine and start searching for new energies and a new life, and she feels herself trying to grasp this inner call and understand what it is telling her. She feels disoriented, but Plato's allegory is starting to work within *her. The imagery of the cave has given her the seed of a new inspiration.*

We can hear this yearning speaking in us in unguarded moments. Yet, somehow we usually remain oblivious to it and behave as if our little "cave" is all there is to life, as if what is missing could be satisfied by modifying our little cave: a raise in salary, a new electronic gadget, a trip abroad. Indeed, this is what our dreams are usually made of: "If only I could get a stable job," "If only I could buy a bigger house with a two-car garage." But, of course, when these dreams come true (if they ever do), we realize that they do not bring us the fullness of life we crave.

Many important philosophical texts serve to remind us of this yearning and to awaken it within us, although it also speaks through literature and poetry, religion and myths, and even in street conversations. Yet, it is in philosophical writings that this yearning is most clearly articulated. Although literary or poetic works might express it beautifully, philosophy can express it with greater clarity. One of philosophy's main tasks is to clarify, articulate, and lay bare the visions that move us.

The Transformational Thinkers

Many thinkers have had the same realization which Plato articulated in his allegory of the cave, namely that we are normally imprisoned in a limited world, and that we need to develop a deeper way of being. They include prominent figures such as Epicurus, Marcus Aurelius, Plotinus, Spinoza, Jean-Jacques Rousseau, Ralph Waldo Emerson, Friedrich Nietzsche, Henri Bergson, Martin Buber, Karl Jaspers, Gabriel Marcel, Krishnamurti, Erich Fromm, and others. This is a very diverse group. Curiously, I know of no philosophy book that groups them together. They belong to different historical periods and different schools of thought, and they employ a variety of ideas, concepts, and methodologies. Nevertheless, they share several powerful themes.

First, these thinkers all suggest that our everyday lives usually remain on a superficial level that does not represent the fullness of human existence. We immerse ourselves in mundane activities—working, shopping, chatting, traveling, relaxing, socializing—believing that this is the way to the good life. But we are mistaken. Our life is governed by a dull routine, by empty moments in which we are hardly conscious, by the power of blind momentum, by distractions and meaningless entertainments, social games, the self-defeating drive to control and acquire and possess. All these leave us distant from ourselves, poor in spirit, isolated from others, disconnected from life.

Second, according to these thinkers there is an alternative way of being that is more faithful to the potential fullness of human reality. It involves not just *doing* something different, but *being* different—being differently with ourselves, with others, with life.

Third, it is not easy to move from our superficial state to a state of fullness. Our natural tendencies do not automatically lead us to it, and overcoming these tendencies is a great challenge. It is not enough to do a workshop twice a week, to read a new theory about life, to do an exercise from six to six-thirty in the morning. Much more is needed: a total transformation that would color every aspect of our being—our emotions, behaviors, thoughts and attitudes, from the smallest moments to the largest deeds.

I call the thinkers who endorse these three themes *transformational thinkers*. Naturally, they express these themes differently. For example, the twentieth-century philosopher Martin Buber[1] articulates them in terms of our relationships to others. He argues that our usual way of relating to those around us is distant and partial. And since he regards relations as central to human existence, he concludes that we are usually not fully true to our reality. A

---

1. Martin Buber, *I and Thou*, New York: Scribner, 1970.

fuller kind of relationship is possible, one which involves real togetherness and is a source of authenticity and life. Another recent thinker, Erich Fromm,[2] focuses on love since according to him love is the main way we overcome our fundamental predicament, namely isolation. He suggests that what we commonly regard as love is not real love, since it is possessive, self-centered, illusory, or otherwise distorted because it maintains our aloneness. In contrast, real love is an attitude of bestowing our plenitude onto the world around us. It involves overflowing towards life—not just towards a specific object of love, and certainly not with the aim of possessing it, but towards the entire world.

Henri Bergson,[3] a prominent French philosopher from the first half of the twentieth century, focuses on our consciousness and the way it flows through time. For him, our usual consciousness expresses only the mechanical surface of our mental life. This surface is composed of fixed, fragmented ideas and emotions that are no longer alive in us, like dead leaves floating on the water of a pond. In order to be truly free and alive, we need to act from the pond itself, from the holistic flow of our life, from the wholeness of our being.

In the nineteenth century, we find the American thinker Ralph Waldo Emerson[4] contending that we usually attain our ideas and motivations from a superficial and restricted self. He urges us to open ourselves to a bigger self, the "Over-Soul," a metaphysical source of plenitude and wisdom that we usually ignore but that can inspire within us a more exalted life.

---

2. Erich Fromm, *The Art of Loving*, New York: Harper & Row, 1956.
3. Henri Bergson, *Time and Free Will: An Essay on the Immediate Data of Consciousness*, New York: Dover Publications, 2001. See especially the section title "The free act."
4. See especially Emerson's essay "The Over-soul" in William Gilman (ed.), *Selected Writings of Ralph Waldo Emerson*, New York: New American Library, 1965, pp. 280-295.

At roughly the same time, Friedrich Nietzsche[5] mocks the herd mentality of those who live a small life of petty concerns, resentment, weakness, submission, and imitation. He calls us to "overcome" our small self and create a higher self and a bigger life by giving birth to our own vision and values, and by striving passionately to live creatively in their light.

Earlier still, in the eighteenth century, Jean-Jacques Rousseau[6] focuses on our dependence on social norms. According to him, we are usually controlled by a social mask—a social self that we acquire as a result of external social pressures. We play social games—mimicking, manipulating, comparing ourselves to others—without realizing that we live an alienated life that is not connected to our real nature. In order to live authentically, we need to connect to our natural self, which is the true fountain of a meaningful life.

In ancient times, the Roman emperor and philosopher Marcus Aurelius[7] tells us that we normally let ourselves be controlled by our automatic emotional reactions, which cling to objects of desire. We are enslaved to our desires to possess and feel good, and so we end up being anxious and frustrated. We can overcome this prison, however, when we detach ourselves from these desires and let ourselves be guided by our inner nature, the rational self, which follows with full acceptance the ways of the cosmos.

Many more examples could be given here: Krishnamurti[8] who calls us to be free from the past and be

---

5. Friedrich Nietzsche, *Thus Spoke Zarathustra*, in Walter Kaufmann (ed.) *The Portable Nietzsche*, New York: Penguin Books, 1978, pp. 103-442. See for example sections 4 and 5 in the "Prologue," pp. 126-131, as well as "On the Three Metamorphoses," in Part 1, pp. 137-140.
6. Jean-Jacques Rousseau, *Emile*, New York: Basic Books, 1979.
7. Marcus Aurelius, *Meditations*, Amherst: Prometheus Books, 1991.
8. See for example Krishnamurti, *The Flight of the Eagle*, New York: Harper & Row, 1971; *The Urgency of Change*, New York: Harper & Row, 1977.

open to the present, Gabriel Marcel[9] who urges us to abandon our remote and alienated state of "observing" and become involved "witnesses" to life, and so on and so forth.

Evidently, these transformational thinkers articulate different ideas, conceive of the human condition in different ways, focus on different aspects of human existence, and even make mutually contradictory statements. Yet, through those diverse ideas they express the same three basic themes: our usual tendency to be in a superficial state, the possibility of a fuller or deeper state, and the challenging transformation that can take us from the former to the latter. These diverse philosophies are, therefore, like different musical variations on the same motif.

Moreover, two additional common themes are common to these transformational approaches. First, they all describe our superficial state as governed by rigid patterns (although they usually do not use the word "pattern")— patterns of behavior, of thought, of desire, of emotions. These patterns are the result of powerful psychological or social mechanisms that operate within us, which lead us to restricted and superficial ways of being that are detached from the fullness of our true reality. To use Plato's imagery, we are imprisoned in a small cave, shackled to our chairs.

Second, all these transformational approaches suggest that the state of fullness is beyond such patterns, and cannot be fitted into any fixed structure. They liken this state to a liberated and open-ended movement, using terms such as freedom, spontaneity, flow, creativity, uniqueness, authenticity, individuality, openness, expansiveness. Interestingly, they describe this free movement only indirectly, without precise analysis. Often they use poetic metaphors or appeal to personal experience, and in general employ indirect means to intimate to the reader what they have in mind. This is hardly surprising. Patterns and mechanisms have a fixed structure and can be analyzed straightforwardly and precisely. In contrast, that which lies

---

9. Gabriel Marcel, "Testimony and Existentialism" in his *The Philosophy of Existentialism*, New Jersey: Citadel Press, 1995, pp. 91-103.

beyond patterns resists analysis, because it overflows any fixed formula.

The Call

We may conclude, therefore, that the various transformational thinkers have been inspired by the same fundamental understanding of human existence. It is not by mere coincidence that their insights are so similar to each other. The vision they all express is based on a common human experience, on a major theme that runs through the fabric of human life. We might say that it is one of the basic dimensions of being human.

However, the word "dimension" might be misleading here because of its scientific connotations. In science and geometry, the term is used to refer to objective aspects of our world. For example, visible space has three dimensions, and this is an objective, neutral fact. In contrast, the transformational thinkers do not present their theories as mere descriptions of neutral human facts. When they speak about the constricted self versus the transformed self, they are not presenting us with a disinterested account of two equally valuable ways of being. Rather, they are telling us that the transformation is something precious and valuable, that we *ought* to seek it. In other words, their theories contain a "call"—a call that tries to grab our attention, to invite us, to urge us to reach out for the fullness of life.

One could say that the transformational thinkers are trying not just to *de*scribe but also to *pre*scribe; not just to depict the way humans *are* but also the way humans *should* be. This does not mean, however, that they are merely expressing their personal preferences. They see themselves as giving voice to a call that pre-existed themselves and their writings, a call they did not invent but rather exposed and articulated. It is not in the name of their personal preferences that they write to us, but in the name of life. From their point of view, the call to live fully comes from the very nature of our human reality. This call has inspired them to write their philosophy, and in a sense is its true author.

We come here to the heart of every philosophical approach that can be called *transformational*: At the center of every such approach is a *call*. It is a call because it nags us, shakes us, pulls away from our comfortable, complacent routine. It invites us, even demands that we try stepping out of our cave and transform ourselves.

We should note, however, that although every transformational philosophy contains such a call, it also contains additional materials—concepts, statements, analyses, explanations, definitions, etc.—and these join together to form a complex theory. Examples of these additional materials are Plato's theory of the world of ideas, Marcus Aurelius' theory of emotions, and Rousseau's theory of education. We might say that in a transformational philosophy, the central call is "clothed" in the garb of a particular theory; or, that the call "speaks through" the medium of a theory.

These theories are of interest to academic philosophers, but for the present investigation they are of lesser interest. For us, it is not the details of the theoretical "clothing" that matter but the essential "body" which these clothes hide— and at the same time reveal. In this book we will try to understand the call which expresses our yearning and which speaks through the various transformational theories, and we will search for ways to incorporate it into our lives.

Chapter 2

The Philosophical Practice Movement

The vision of self-transformation is lofty and attractive, but the question is how to translate it into practice. What should we do if we wish to step out of our Platonic cave?

The answer given by most of the transformational philosophers throughout the ages is: philosophy, or more accurately, philosophizing, in other words, the activity of philosophical reflection. Philosophical reflection can help us understand the meaning of our yearning, it can help us examine our life and see its narrowness, it can inspire us to envision a deeper kind of life, it can show us what such a life would require, and give us some tools for self-transformation.

This might sound strange. Philosophy nowadays is largely limited to university courses and academic articles and is typically focused on abstract, impersonal ideas. How can such ideas possibly make a practical difference to our daily life?

The answer is that ideas are not powerless, even if they seem abstract. Ideas—ideas in general, not just philosophical ones—have a tremendous power to change us. New understandings can awaken within us new motivations, inspire us to feel and behave in new ways, and cultivate in us new attitudes and energies. For example, a social vision about the suffering of the poor may inspire a person to start devoting time and energies to helping the needy; an ecological awareness about the fragility of the environment may make a person start behaving respectfully towards nature and natural resources; an existential realization about the inevitability of death can motivate an individual to start appreciating the preciousness of the present moment; a religious realization can inspire a person to be meek and loving. Not only grand visions of life influence us. Our daily behavior is constantly shaped by our understanding of what the boss expects us to do, by our understanding of our financial situation, of our moral obligations, of what is best for our children, or what others think about us.

But although many kinds of understandings influence our life, for the task of self-transformation, philosophical reflection is especially promising. Philosophical reflection examines the foundation of our life, the concepts that lie at the very basis of our everyday attitudes. It can, therefore, influence not just a specific behavior, but our entire orientation towards life. Furthermore, philosophical reflection, by its very nature, is a critical and open-ended investigation, and it can, therefore, show us our boundaries and limitations—the walls of our "cave"—and question them. Unlike dogmas and doctrines that want us to follow them blindly, philosophizing encourages us to question every assumption, to take nothing for granted, to explore new ways of understanding, and to step into uncharted terrains. Dogmas and doctrines are like Platonic "caves" which imprison us in a rigid attitude, while a philosophical investigation is a journey that can lead us outside our prison, to a broader worldview, to a wider scope of life.

Many transformational thinkers throughout the history of philosophy believed that philosophical reflection can help in the quest for a fuller life, but in modern times this realization has been largely neglected. Most professional philosophers nowadays prefer theoretical discussions to practical philosophy. They usually treat age-old transformational visions as mere intellectual ideas, without any serious attempt to implement them into practice. Rarely do they translate them into daily exercises, for example, or into self-development workshops for their students.

Philosophy has not always been a purely intellectual endeavor. Practical approaches to philosophy can be found in ancient Greek and Hellenistic schools (roughly from the 6th century BC to the 4th century AD) which viewed philosophy as a way of life.[10] But from a contemporary perspective, they have their limitations. Although they translated their ideas to concrete guidelines for everyday behaviors and emotions, their approaches were rather dogmatic. Each philosophical school had a specific doctrine about life, and it tried to direct disciples into accepting its tenets and following them. To be sure, the founders of these schools were deep and creative philosophers, but to their disciples they gave an already-finished philosophical system to follow. These disciples were encouraged to reflect only within the boundary of this system, not to diverge from it, not to seriously question its principles, not to embark on a free and open philosophical search.

Such dogmatism is too restrictive nowadays, and in fact is just like another Platonic cave. For us today it is hard to accept that one single doctrine can capture the whole of reality. If we wish to use philosophy in the journey towards self-transformation, we need a broader philosophical approach, more pluralistic and open-ended, with no final answers and no rigid doctrines.

Practical approaches to philosophy can also be found in the Orient, in many schools of Hinduism, Buddhism, Confucianism, Taoism, among others. But these spiritual and philosophical schools, too, are typically committed to specific religious or metaphysical doctrines, and they are therefore less relevant to the idea of philosophy as a personal, open-ended journey that takes nothing for granted and is willing to question any given assumption.

Philosophizing versus philosophical theories

We come here to an important distinction between two different notions that are often confused: *philosophical*

10. Pierre Hadot, *Philosophy as a Way of Life: Spiritual Exercises from Socrates to Foucault*, Malden, MA: Blackwell, 1995.

reflection or *philosophizing* on the one hand, and *a philosophy* on the other (note the article "a" preceding the word "philosophy"). *Philosophical reflection,* or *philosophizing,* is an activity. It is an open investigation which searches without preconception, without taking for granted any assumption or principle. It is what true philosophers do.

In contrast, *a philosophy* is a finished theory. It lays down certain principles and ideas and declares them to be true. A philosophy is a product of a philosopher's philosophical reflection. For example, Plato's theory of knowledge is a philosophy—it is the product of the philosophical reflection which he had conducted. Kant's theory of knowledge is another philosophy—it is the product of the philosophical reflection conducted by Kant.

Philosophical theories can help us see how great minds think, and they are worth studying carefully. They can teach us how to think deeply, they can offer us concepts and ideas which we can adopt to our own thinking, and they can inspire us to develop our own philosophical reflections. As raw materials for us to examine, modify, adopt or reject, they are powerful. But if we take them as final truths, as a gospel to accept and revere, then we are being dogmatic. While philosophizing opens us, accepting a philosophy as an authority closes our thinking.

Any philosophy as a fixed dogma is not likely to lead us out of our Platonic cave since it erects fixed assumptions and boundaries. In contrast, a philosophical reflection—the process of philosophizing, or of free and open philosophical exploration—has the potential of taking us beyond our boundaries.

What is philosophizing?

We cannot hope for an exact definition of a complex activity such as philosophizing, much less a definition that would be agreed by all. In the history of philosophy we find many different ways of philosophizing. Nevertheless, it is possible to identify several central themes that are common to most forms of philosophizing, at least in the West.

Philosophizing is what philosophers have been doing throughout the ages. What is it that they have been doing?

When we look at the important philosophers throughout the ages, we can find at least five themes that are undoubtedly common to virtually all of them.

First, all philosophers address fundamental issues of reality, especially fundamental issues of life. They all investigate issues that are at the very foundation of our understanding of ourselves, our life, and the world: What is knowledge? What is matter? What is love? What is the good life? What is morally right and morally wrong? And so on. Saying that such issues are fundamental implies, among other things, that they are general issues of existence, not limited to the specific condition of John or of Mary. If you only discuss John's specific love story or Mary's specific family problem, then you are not yet philosophizing.

Second, all philosophers try to address those fundamental issues by developing theories, or more generally networks of ideas. They do not satisfy themselves with writing a one-sentence slogan, or an arbitrary list of unrelated statements, or a story about John or Mary. Rather, they develop a network of ideas that connect together in complex ways into a coherent whole, designed to offer a certain understanding of the issue. This is not the only way to address basic issues of existence. One can also address them through poetry, literature, painting, religious faith or political action. But philosophers philosophize in order to gain an understanding of these issues by articulating coherent bodies of ideas.

Third, philosophers construct those networks of ideas not on the basis of faith or personal conviction (as in religion), not on the basis of scientific experiments (as in psychology, for example, or biology), but on the basis of thinking, or reasoning. Reasoning does not necessarily mean logical thinking in the strict sense since some philosophers use so-called poetic reasoning, or intuitive thinking. Also, reasoning does not mean conclusive proofs—no final proof is possible in philosophical issues. Nevertheless, all true philosophers try to support their ideas with considerations that make them as coherent, tenable and compelling as possible. Once a thinker makes claims dogmatically, arbitrarily, without attempting to support them with any kind of reason, he or she is outside the territory of philosophy.

Fourth, all philosophers construct their ideas in a creative process. They do not simply copy ideas from some gospel or from another philosopher. They create their own novel, original ideas. This means that merely reading a philosophical book, or analyzing somebody else's ideas does not in itself amount to philosophizing.

But fifth, philosophers are not isolated from other thinkers. Almost invariably they develop their ideas through dialogue with other thinkers, whether in face-to-face meetings, written correspondence, or inner dialogues with the writings of past thinkers. Philosophical reflection is not born in a vacuum, but always in a context of a historical discourse. It is not a coincidence that Aristotle developed his philosophy in response to the philosophy of his teacher Plato, and that Immanuel Kant developed his philosophical ideas in response to those of the British philosopher David Hume.

To sum up, to philosophize is, as a first approximation, to investigate basic issues of existence by creating networks of ideas in a reasoned, creative, and dialogical way. Therefore, when we say that philosophizing can help us step out of the Platonic cave, we are in effect saying that reflecting philosophically on basic life-issues can be a way of personal growth and self-transformation.

Notice that it is the *process* of philosophizing that is said here to transform us, not a fixed philosophical doctrine. The point is not that some philosophical theory by Plato or Nietzsche can tell us how to transform ourselves. Philosophizing, by its very essence, rejects any guru, any doctrine, any final authority. In order to step out of our Platonic cave, we need to engage in our own personal philosophical exploration, not to simply accept an existing philosophical guideline and follow it blindly. It is the philosophical search that has the power to lead us to discover our personal boundaries and expand ourselves beyond them into new depths and new horizons.

The philosophical practice movement

The vision which I am proposing above, of philosophizing as a way to self-transformation, is a product of a long process. I have been developing it and experimenting with it over the past two-and-a-half decades in which I have been actively involved in the *philosophical practice* movement. Philosophical practice is a contemporary movement that is inspired by the vision that philosophical reflection is relevant to our everyday lives. It can be seen as a modern attempt to revive the mission of the ancient philosophical schools of life while avoiding their dogmatism. It seeks to help individuals reflect on themselves, examine their predicaments, develop a better self-understanding, and deal more deeply with their fundamental life-issues.

Philosophical reflection in this sense does not seek to theorize in the abstract about life, but to be woven into life. It is therefore fundamentally different from mainstream academic philosophy. The academic philosopher is somebody who theorizes—somebody who writes articles and books, discusses, lectures, and produces abstract theories. In contrast, philosophical practitioners seek to impregnate life—their own life and the lives of others— with philosophical reflection. They therefore have a great interest in the concrete situation and concrete concerns of individual persons. Although they may occasionally theorize in the abstract, they do so only as a means for something else: helping people find the way to live life more fully, deeply, and wisely.

At the same time, philosophical practice is also different from so-called "applied philosophy," which has become popular in universities in the past several decades. Applied philosophy typically takes the form of applied ethics (how to apply general ethical considerations to specific ethical dilemmas) business ethics (how to apply general ethical considerations to specific business situations), and similar sub-fields. It attempts to *apply* abstract ideas to concrete situations. For example, it develops abstract ethical principles and then applies them to specific medical dilemmas. Philosophical practice, in contrast, is not interested in imposing ideas on life. It wants our understandings to grow in the midst of life.

The philosophical practice movement was born in the early 1980s when Gerd Achenbach opened his philosophical practice in Germany. He started giving counseling sessions to individuals, and also founded a philosophy reflection group. This in itself was not an innovation—many philosophers throughout history had used philosophy to help individuals reflect on life-issues. But he was the first to found a professional association devoted to this endeavor. A year later, a second group was formed in Holland by philosophy students from the University of Amsterdam. Inspired by Achenbach's example but working quite independently of him, they experimented with philosophical counseling to individuals and with discussion groups. Soon afterwards they formed their own association.

For more than a decade, the new field of philosophical practice was largely limited to those two small groups in Germany and in Holland. Only a handful of other individuals were experimenting in other countries. In 1992, when I heard of the new fledgling movement—I was then a young philosophy professor at a university in the USA—my reaction was like that of many other philosophers when they first heard about it: "Of course! What can be a better guide to living than philosophy!?" The idea resonated with many thoughts I had had years earlier during my philosophy and psychology studies, when as a student I deplored the excessive intellectualism of academic philosophy and its remoteness from everyday life.

I started experimenting myself with philosophical counseling, at first counseling volunteers and then paying clients. I also communicated with the two European groups, read their writings, and traveled a couple of times to Europe to meet them. I soon realized that philosophical practice was still in its infancy, still trying to find what philosophical practice was all about. I decided that the new movement needed a serious international dialogue, and I envisioned an international conference that would involve philosophers from a variety of backgrounds and orientations. I tried to interest several universities to host such a conference, but at first nobody wanted to invest in this unknown field. I also started publishing articles in professional journals about philosophical practice and began editing an anthology—a collection of articles by leading practitioners, primarily German and Dutch, which was soon published as a book.[11]

Shortly afterwards, one of the contributors to the anthology, Lou Marinoff, who was then a young professor at the University of British Columbia in Canada, suggested that we try his university. And indeed, the two of us managed to convince his superior, the head of the Center for Applied Ethics, and in 1994 we launched the First International Conference of Philosophical Counseling. More than a hundred philosophers from about ten countries came to participate, and many new ideas were discussed. Since then international conferences have been taking place in different countries, usually once every two years.

As a result of this conference, and probably other factors as well, the idea started spreading. Philosophers in other countries started experimenting with philosophical practice, often without knowing how exactly it was being practiced in Germany and Holland, due to language barriers and geographical distance. They explored the idea individually or in groups, in North America, in Israel, and soon afterwards in most West European countries, as well as in several Latin American countries. As a consequence, a wide variety of approaches started to develop in different parts of the world.

All this resulted in a network of loosely connected groups and individuals who have different goals and methods, speak different languages, have different

---

11. *Essays on Philosophical Counseling*, edited by Ran Lahav and Maria Tillmanns, Lanham: University Press of America, 1995.

publications, and yet see themselves as part of the same international movement and as inspired by the same vision: to make philosophical reflection relevant to the individual's life. The field is, therefore, varied and pluralistic. Many local groups and associations operate today in numerous countries. They are involved in counseling individuals and organizations, giving workshops and training courses, organizing philosophical cafés, and publishing newsletters and journals. In the past decade, several universities have started offering courses and programs devoted to the field.[12]

To add to the complexity of the field, philosophical practice functions in several different formats. For example, it is sometimes practiced as a *philosophical self-reflection workshop* that is offered to the general public, where, under the guidance of a philosophical practitioner, participants reflect philosophically on their personal experiences and predicaments. Alternatively, philosophical practice is also practiced in the form of a *philosophical discussion group* of various kinds, especially the so-called *philosophical café* and *Socratic Dialogue groups*, in which participants develop their personal thinking about various life-issues. It can also be practiced in the form of a *philosophical companionship*: a group of companions who meet over a period of time, online or face to face, and contemplate in togetherness on a philosophical text while trying to do so from their inner depth. Another format is the *personal philosophical journey*, which is practiced by an individual philosophical seeker. But perhaps the most popular format nowadays is still *philosophical counseling*. As its name implies, philosophical counseling involves a philosopher who serves as a counselor, and a counselee. The two meet periodically and discuss the counselee's predicaments, dilemmas, and life. Typically, the counseling sessions are about one-hour

---

12. As far as I know, the first university course on the topic was taught by me at Haifa University in Israel, one semester a year between 1993-2006. Courses on philosophical practice are also being given at the University of Venice, Roma Tre in Rome, University of Barcelona, University of Sevilla, University of Vienna, and others.

long, they are held once or twice a week, and they may continue anywhere from a single session to many months, depending on the counselor's approach and the counselee's needs.

In all those diverse formats, philosophical practice is centered on philosophizing with individuals about basic life-issues, and on how those life-issues are expressed in their personal lives. This is why it is a form of philosophizing and not of psychology. Philosophy, after all, deals with ideas. The philosophical practitioner helps individuals explore their hidden assumptions, uncover the values which motivate them, examine their conceptions of life, and reflect on the coherence and tenability of their worldview. During the session, they often examine together ideas of relevant historical thinkers or read together a philosophical text in order to enrich the conversation and deepen the emerging insights. Philosophical practitioners must, therefore, have a broad philosophical background, and it is generally expected that they must have at least a Master's degree in philosophy.

Different approaches to philosophical practice

What exactly do philosophical practitioners do in their sessions? And what is their aim?

As mentioned earlier, philosophical practice, like many other fields, is not a single unified approach. Different approaches exist today, representing different views about what philosophy can contribute to our lives. Despite this variety, it seems that most philosophical practices can be divided into several main groups, in accordance with their goal and in accordance with their methods.

In terms of their goal, the different forms of philosophical practice can be divided into three main groups. First, there are those practices that can be put under the label of the *Problem-Solving Approach*. These practices help individuals address specific problems in their lives and overcome them: dissatisfaction at work, marital difficulties, low self-esteem, etc.[13] In this respect, they bear some resemblance to psychologists from the school of cognitive psychotherapy. A related approach attempts to help individuals develop thinking skills with which they could address in the future personal problems and challenges. The emphasis in this *Thinking Skills Approach* is on developing thinking tools, instead of solving specific issues, but the emphasis is still on practical means of addressing everyday concerns. A third group of philosophical practices, which can be labeled the *Self-Development Approach*, aim at enriching life with greater meaning and wisdom, making life fuller, or in short edifying life.[14]

I have already hinted that I sympathize with the self-development approach when I suggested that philosophy can be used to facilitate self-transformation. Philosophy deals with fundamental life-issues, and it is at its best when it helps individuals grapple with the basic issues of life. Rather than lowering philosophy to the level of everyday concerns, philosophical practice should seek to elevate life to the heights of its potentials.

Of course, philosophy might also prove useful in dealing with concrete personal concerns, such as marital problems or tensions at the workplace, but this seems to jar with the spirit of the philosophical tradition. A philosophy that aims at problem solving is basically a satisfaction-provider. It aims at making people content so that they could go back to their normal lives. This kind of practice is obviously very different from the vision that inspired the great philosophers throughout the ages, who sought to *question* "normal" life rather than to promote it. Socrates, Rousseau,

---

13. See for example Lou Marinoff, *Plato, Not Prozac*, New York: HarperCollins, 1999; Elliot Cohen, *What Would Aristotle Do?*, Amherst, NY: Prometheus, 2003.
14. See Gerd Achenbach, "Philosophy, Philosophical Practice, and Psychotherapy," in Ran Lahav and Maria Tillmanns (eds.), *Essays on Philosophical Counseling*, Lanham: University Press of American, 1995, pp. 61-74; "Philosophical Counseling and Self-Transformation," in Elliot Cohen (ed.), *Philosophy, Counseling, and Psychotherapy*, Cambridge Scholars Press, 2013.

or Nietzsche tried to awaken people from their slumber, to questions their comfortable assumptions, to shake them up with new insights, not to normalize them back to their daily slumber. One should hope that philosophy can do greater things than making people content.

One might call those philosophical practices which aim at addressing personal problems *small philosophical practice*, because they give philosophy a limited task—to deal with specific elements within life, rather than examine the foundation of life. The name also indicates that the aspirations of such a practice are limited: producing satisfaction. In contrast, the goal of philosophical practice as I see it is not to solve and satisfy, but rather to awaken forgotten dissatisfactions and yearnings, to transcend our everyday needs, arouse wonder, awe, even confusion, and in this way open for us new doors towards greater horizons of understanding and life.

That is not to say that small philosophical practices should be rejected. If philosophy can be used to make people more satisfied, then there is nothing wrong with that. But this kind of practice has little to do with philosophy in its traditional and deeper sense, that of the search for a life of wisdom.

So much for dividing philosophical practices according to their goal. But they can also be divided in accordance with their method, and here we can discern two main groups. First, there are those philosophical practices that emphasize rational analysis, or more generally critical thinking.[15] Proponents of this *Critical Thinking Approach* believe that philosophy is essentially an endeavor of rational analysis. Therefore, the methods of philosophical counseling must be based on logical thinking tools such as formulating arguments, detecting logical validity and fallacies, analyzing concepts, exposing hidden assumptions, or what is collectively called "critical thinking." Critical thinking can presumably be used to help individuals

---

15. See especially Elliot Cohen, *What Would Aristotle Do?*, Amherst, NY: Prometheus, 2003.

analyze their personal problems, their behavior, beliefs, and even emotions.

This approach seems to me to suffer from several serious problems. First, from twenty-six centuries of philosophy it takes only tools of logical thinking while ignoring all other philosophical treasures. It does not utilize the rich, complex body of philosophical ideas which have been developed throughout the ages, but satisfies itself only with the tools of rational analysis. This seems to me an unfortunate impoverishment of philosophy's potential contribution to life. Excessive focus on the technical "how" is bound to leave out the more important "what" of great philosophies.

Second, the idea that critical thinking is a central component in the philosophies of the great thinkers is very questionable. Virtually all philosophers throughout history did much more than apply logical skills to analyze ideas: They *created* ideas, constructing complex and magnificent theories to shed light on basic life-issues. Their work was inspired by world-visions, and it was nourished by creativity and imagination, rather than being limited to dry, technical, logical skills.

Third, critical thinking does not seem special to philosophy—any serious academic discipline uses it. Lawyers, economists, politicians, and psychologists use critical thinking no less than philosophers. The fact that a given practice uses critical thinking does not make it philosophical.

The alternative to the critical thinking approach is what can be called the *Wisdom Approach*. Here the focus is not on rational analysis and critical thinking (although these too may play a role), but rather on deep philosophical ideas. Its main task is not to analyze ideas, but to create and construct ideas, because it seeks to develop rich understandings of life. This approach utilizes the treasures of wisdom from the history of philosophy, although not as authorities to follow but as sources of inspiration for personal exploration and growth.

It is evident from everything I have said so far that my own approach is aimed at the goal self-development (in the form of self-transformation), and that it seeks wisdom which goes much beyond critical thinking. This is the approach which I will present in this book, and which grew out of my activity as a philosophical practitioner.

Philosophical Practice versus Psychology

The idea that philosophy can help us understand ourselves and live a fuller life might seem to be an infringement upon the boundaries of psychology. Isn't it the business of the psychologist to deal with our personal predicaments?

I cannot speak in the name of all philosophical practitioners. In my view, there are indeed many philosophical practitioners who use psychological methods and ideas in their practice. What they do, in my opinion, is not really a philosophical kind of practice but rather psychological counseling with a few philosophical elements mixed in. In this respect, what they do is not very different from cognitive psychotherapy, existential psychotherapy, or other philosophy-oriented psychologies that are common today. This seems to me a pity, since it dilutes the great potentials of philosophizing and misses its unique powers of philosophizing, which are very different from psychologizing.

In any case, since I can speak here only for myself, from now on I will discuss only my own philosophical vision and my own approach to practicing philosophy. Let me start with a historical perspective.

Psychology is a very young field, relative to philosophy's long history. Philosophy in the West is 2600 years old, while psychology, as a separate field with scientific aspirations, emerged only at the end of the nineteenth century and early twentieth century. Prior to the birth of psychology, the study of human emotion, cognition, and behavior had been part of philosophy. Major philosophers throughout the ages investigated the human psyche, classifying mental states, explaining psychological processes, exploring the sources of emotions and thoughts, their function and their interrelationships.

At about the same time that psychology broke away from philosophy to become a science, around the end of the nineteenth century, an applied form of psychology appeared on the scene: psychological therapy, or the "talking cure." It quickly grew to become a major profession in our contemporary world and to gain a nearly complete monopoly over the treatment of personal predicaments. Sigmund Freud was a major pioneer and contributor to the consolidation of psychology as a therapy of the soul. The new field soon began splitting into types and sub-types ("psychoanalysis," "cognitive psychotherapy," humanistic psychotherapy," etc.), but for the sake of simplicity I will regard all of them as forms of "psychotherapy."

Psychotherapists today are regarded as professionals: They are equipped with theories about the workings of human emotions and behavior and with methods of intervention, they have been trained to develop the necessary sensitivity to interact with clients, and the skills to analyze personal problems and help resolve them. In this sense, the rise of psychotherapy in the past century can be seen as a transition from the wisdom-based endeavor of traditional philosophy to a new skill-based and science-based endeavor, from the wise person to the professional, from visions of life to professional theories and techniques. In today's technological world, which has a higher regard for skill and professionalism than for wisdom, it is no wonder that the psychotherapist is acknowledged as an authority on personal predicaments. The modern movement of philosophical practice can be seen as a call to return to the ways of wisdom.

All this, however, is an oversimplification. Psychotherapy nowadays is not one single thing but is composed of hundreds of different approaches, and any generalization is bound to do injustice to some of them. Some psychological approaches contain philosophical elements, and as such they are not completely outside the boundaries of philosophy. Indeed, they partially overlap with certain forms of philosophical practice. This is not surprising, because most fields nowadays have considerable overlap with other fields: Physicists often step into the territory of chemistry, chemists into biology, social psychologists into sociology. We cannot reasonably expect a clear dividing line between the practice of philosophers and the practice of psychologists. It would be better, therefore, to draw a distinction not between what psychologists do and what philosophical practitioners do, but rather between psychological ways of thinking and philosophical ways of thinking, regardless of whether they take place in the psychologist's office or in the philosopher's office.

From the perspective of my own approach, there are several fundamental differences between these two:

First, as its name implies, psychology works with the psyche. It deals with *processes* or *mechanisms* in the individual's life which shape their emotions, thoughts, behaviors, attitudes. In contrast, philosophy works primarily with *ideas*. Philosophical practice, as a form of philosophizing, is based on the realization that ideas have a tremendous power to move us and transform our lives.

Evidence for this power can be seen, as noted earlier, when a person undergoes a profound transformation under the inspiration of a social vision, an insight about themselves, or a new existential awareness of death. The problem is that influential ideas are not necessarily profound and beneficial; in fact, they are sometimes dogmatic and shallow, narrowing life rather than broadening it. Examples are rigid religious doctrines, or racist ideologies used to brainwash the individual. The challenge is, therefore, to find ways to inspire individuals with ideas that can open and deepen and enrich. Philosophy, which is a critical and open-ended exploration of fundamental life-issues, is the natural means to this end.

Philosophy is not interested in every idea which people happen to have. It is not interested in average opinions or popular ways of thinking—these are of interest to the psychologist or sociologist. It is not interested in how people *normally* think, but rather in *potential* ways of thinking which express coherence, depth, meaning, wisdom. This implies a second basic difference between the two practices. Psychology, as a study of how people feel, think, and behave, focuses on the range of *actual* human functions. In contrast, philosophical practice is primarily interested in the higher dimensions of existence, those dimensions which are rare and often hidden. The main task of psychotherapy is to make human life functional and satisfying in relation to normal human life, while the mission of philosophical practice (as I see it) is to rise above normality, above functionality, seeking that which is precious and even profound.

In this respect, philosophical practice as I see it is similar to the ancient schools of philosophy in the West, such as Stoicism and Neo-Platonism. They, too, were interested not in resolving personal problems and restoring normal human functions, but in leading people to go beyond their usual state and attain higher ways of being.

It follows that the qualifications required for practicing the two practices are also very different. Psychologists need to have the capacity to deal with normal and abnormal human conditions. This includes knowledge of normal and abnormal human functions and predicaments, sensitivity to people, and skills to analyze human situations and use intervention techniques. Philosophical practitioners, in contrast, need to be experienced travelers in the realm of ideas. They must have a broad knowledge of historical conceptions of basic life-issues, a good capacity to creatively develop ideas, and the wisdom and life experience to relate to the higher dimensions of human existence. In short, one might say by way of a crude generalization that psychology deals with life as we see it around us, while philosophical practice seeks to travel to the farthest and most profound horizons of human existence.

Jenny seems to have everything—a well-paying job, a loving husband, an upper-middle-class lifestyle, two well-

adjusted children, and many friends. For ten years she had been working hard as a free-lance journalist, until a few months ago she finally found a stable job with a respectable magazine. And yet, she is now starting to feel that something is missing in her life, she doesn't know what. At times she is gripped by a vague anxiety and a sense that she is wasting her life. Discussing her childhood with her therapist doesn't seem to help much.

"It appears to me," the therapist eventually says, "that you don't want me to 'cure' you of your dissatisfaction. In fact, you don't really need a cure."

"What do you mean? I feel emptiness, and it weighs on me almost day by day."

"Let's imagine, Jenny, that I could give you a miracle pill that would make your dissatisfaction disappear. It would take you back to your normal life, and you would feel content just as you used to two or three years ago. Would you take this pill?"

"No," Jenny admits. "I don't want to go back to what you call my 'normal' life. Frankly, I don't find my 'normal' life appealing anymore. It needs a big change."

"Exactly," the therapist concludes. "You are dissatisfied not because of some psychological problem, but because you are yearning to grow, to expand your life. Why don't you try changing your career? Or taking a sabbatical and touring the world? Or, better still, go see a philosophical counselor?"

Jenny starts seeing a philosophical counselor. Through their conversations she discovers that, like most other people, she is a prisoner of certain ideas about how life is supposed to be. Her personal Platonic "cave" is, in part, her implicit assumption that the goal of life is having a family and a career. Presumably, once you have a well-functioning family and a well-paying job, your life should be meaningful. This idea, which she has always taken for granted without even putting it into words, has been motivating her to work hard, almost obsessively, and has been directing her behavior, attitudes, hopes, and plans. Now that she has achieved her goal of having a stable job, she is realizing that it is not enough for her.

"Alright," Jenny says, "I am starting to see my boundaries—in theory. But practically speaking, how do I step out of them?"

"Not so fast," Linda the philosophical counselor replies. "Before stepping out, you need to understand more deeply what you are stepping out of."

"You mean my childhood experiences, defense mechanisms, and all that?"

"No, Jenny, we are not doing psychotherapy. In philosophy we reflect on ideas—ideas about life, about what it means to live fully, about what is important and precious. We work on understanding their deeper meaning, and what they might mean to you personally. To some extent, I can help you do it. But in addition, we have 2,500 years worth of writings from the great minds who have already developed many ideas about basic life-issues, and some of them might give you insights and inspiration to develop your own new path."

Linda now introduces into the discussion several passages from the ancient philosopher Epicurus, hoping that they would help give Jenny a new perspective on herself. Jenny is intrigued by Epicurus' distinction between true needs (true desires) and false needs (false desires), and his contention that most of the things we think we need are not true needs."

"But what is a true need, then?" Jenny objects.

"That's an excellent question, Jenny. Let's think about it together."

"Well, Epicurus seems to have a definite answer to this question."

"Indeed he does."

"I think he is saying that fancy things beyond basic existence are not true needs. For him, we don't really need much money over and above what's necessary for a painless survival. We don't need expensive clothes or bigger homes. And if I apply this to modern life, we don't really need new electronic gadgets or fancy cars."

Linda, the philosophical counselor, nods in agreement. Jenny adds: "But why did you want me to read this? I don't *buy fancy stuff, I am not very much interested in luxury. This may be a problem for other people, but not for me!"*

"I understand, Jenny. But let's go deeper. Beyond the specific details of his philosophy, Epicurus gives us a general test to decide which of our desires is based on a true need and which of our desires is based on a false need."

"A general test?"

"Yes. A general criterion to assess our desires, or our wants."

"You mean that true desires are those that make us happy?"

"Precisely. A need, or a want, is true if its satisfaction is likely to give you happiness, or what he calls pleasure. Epicurus means a quiet, painless state of mind, without anxiety or distress."

Jenny ponders. "No, I don't think I like this. I am not looking to be content or even happy. I want to feel that I am doing something... I don't know, something meaningful."

"Excellent. So by way of disagreeing with Epicurus, you are now starting to develop your own understanding of true needs. That's the nice thing about deep thinkers: They inspire you to think by yourself even when you disagree with them. In fact, agreeing or disagreeing with them is not the point at all."

"Alright, so where do we go from here?"

"You say, Jenny, that what you truly need, what you are truly after, is not a feeling of happiness, but doing something meaningful. Now, what sort of things do you think are meaningful?"

A conversation ensues. They do not delve into Jenny's psychology—into her hidden desires or unconscious anxieties or childhood experiences, as a psychologist might do. The two focus not on Jenny's existing wants, but on her potential wants, those wants she does not yet have but might be worth having. The issue of what is meaningful has little to do with Jenny's psychology.

In the next two sessions, the counselor and counselee continue to discuss this issue, and they also relate to Jenny's past attitudes to life and what she had been pursuing in recent years. Jenny realizes that she always had definite wants and goals—a "solid" career and a "solid" home as she puts it—and had been pursuing them with much devotion, without ever questioning them. She had never asked herself whether these goals were worth pursuing and what they were likely to do to her life. She had never considered the possibility of alternative goals worth pursuing.

Every once in a while Linda brings into to the conversation additional relevant philosophies of true wants and of meaningfulness. She mentions Herbert Marcuse's view of true needs as liberating from repressive social structures of which the individual is often unaware. She also mentions William James' view that a meaningful activity is one which involves a struggle to fulfill a personal ideal.

"Not everything these thinkers say resonates with me," Jenny muses after a long conversation that combines personal experiences and abstract ideas. "But what I take away from them is the insight that my goals impact my inner life. The goals I pursue shape the kind of person I am. I should think more about my inner life, not just about the things I do and achieve."

"It's good, Jenny, that you are not taking any of these thinkers as a gospel. They are only specific voices in a rich choir of life. But where does your conclusion take us? You want to develop your inner life—but how? If you could choose freely, what sort of inner life would you want?"

"Well... I don't know yet. I can't think of any way to answer this question."

In the following session, Linda presents three brief philosophical texts, and she explains each of them in a few words. At first she explains the passionate self-creation of Nietzsche's "overman"; then Emerson's openness to an inner fountain of inspiration; and finally Bergson's holistic and creative symphony of experiences. In the following sessions, Linda helps Jenny reflect on how these philosophies might relate to her everyday life, but she also encourages her to modify them in any way she likes.

As Jenny examines herself through the lens of these ideas, she gains new insights about herself. She now

*understands that she had been suffocating in her narrow
conception of what life is about, and that she longs to
expand. New perspectives on human experience start
unfolding for her and inspiring her. Although she continues
with her job, she feels the beginning of a new inner change.*

*"I've come to realize that I can be broader inside—yes,
'broader' is the word that resonates in me, although I still
cannot define it accurately. But even without a definition, I
feel that something inside me has been constricted for a
long time. And I know it doesn't have to be this way."*

*She decides not to be worried about defining the words
she is starting to use in her own unique way: "broad,"
"narrow," expand," "shrunk." As Linda says, she is in the
process of giving birth to her own vision of life, and it would
take time and a lot of self-reflection and experimentation to
make her vision clear to herself.*

Jenny's case illustrates how different philosophical
practice is from the psychotherapist's work on
psychological materials. In philosophical practice, the
philosopher and the counselee work primarily with ideas
about human existence, especially those that relate to the
higher dimensions of life—something most psychologists
would regard as a diversion from the real issues. According
to many forms of psychotherapy, the real issues are
psychological materials that influence the individual's well-
being: childhood experiences and defense mechanisms (in
depth-psychology), belief-systems (in cognitive therapy),
feelings about oneself (in person-centered therapy), and so
on. In contrast, for the philosopher, materials that are in the
person's psyche are not of prime interest. Philosophy is
about ideas.

To be sure, psychologists too use ideas (or theories) in
their work, but primarily as tools for their work rather than
as something to discuss with their clients. For example, a
Freudian analyst might *use* a theory about repressed
stressful experiences, and a cognitive psychotherapist
might *use* a theory about how beliefs influence emotions,
but they don't discuss and analyze these psychological

theories with their clients. Likewise, person-centered therapists might *make use* of the idea that unconditional acceptance promotes growth, but the therapy itself does not consist in explaining this idea to clients and discussing it together. For the psychotherapist, psychological theories are tools to work with, not topics for discussion in the psychotherapy session.

In contrast, in philosophical practice the discussion of ideas (concepts, theories, premises, arguments, etc.) is at the center of the process. No theory is taken for granted. Any theory that is brought up is open for discussion, modification or rejection.

It may be objected that some forms of psychotherapy do incorporate discussions of ideas with clients. And this is correct only in a limited sense. Cognitive therapists, for example, discuss various issues with their clients, but the discussion is a technique for influencing clients towards "positive" thoughts or "functional" behaviors. Discussions are not meant to enrich the clients' world, but rather to influence them in a pre-determined direction. In the process, clients are directed towards simplistic views of life and practical solutions, rather than towards complex, deep, and even confusing horizons of understanding. In contrast, the philosophical discussion is a truly open-ended investigation, and it is guided by a genuine attempt to develop richer and deeper understandings of life.

Perhaps the most philosophically oriented form of psychotherapy is existential therapy (and existential counseling). Existential psychotherapy is based on the views of important existentialist philosophers—Friedrich Nietzsche, Karl Jaspers, Martin Heidegger, Jean-Paul Sartre, and others—who portrayed the human condition as an open, ongoing task. According to these thinkers, to be fully human means to struggle with life's basic issues, especially the search for meaning, the attempt to be authentic, the need to fully acknowledge one's freedom and responsibility, one's fundamental aloneness, and one's upcoming death. These philosophical ideas have been adopted by existential psychotherapies as their theoretical basis. A powerful example is Irvin Yalom, an influential American existentialist psychiatrist, whose approach is based on the view that people typically struggle with four main basic life-issues (or basic "givens": freedom, isolation, meaning, and death), which are at the root of most personal predicaments.[16]

In some limited sense, this kind of therapy is philosophical since it relates to life-issues that have been the subject matter of many philosophical discussions. On the other hand, it is not fully philosophical because it is committed to a specific theory, namely existentialism. It takes existentialism as a doctrine, as the foundation of therapy, and not as one possible philosophy among many others to discuss. Within the session there is not much room for questioning the existentialist assumptions, or seriously considering alternative conceptions of life, certainly not with the client. For this reason, existentialist psychotherapy, though containing certain philosophical elements, does not employ true philosophizing with clients, as philosophical practice does.

Just as a given psychotherapy may contain philosophical elements, a philosophical practice may contain psychotherapeutic elements to the extent that it takes into account the client's psychological processes and mechanisms. Indeed, awareness of both the psychological and the philosophical perspectives is helpful, since these are two important dimensions of life that cannot be ignored.

---

16. *Love's Executioner*, New York: Basic Books, 1988. See especially the Prologue.

Chapter 3

Our Platonic Cave – the Perimeter

So far I have been speaking very generally about the "Platonic cave" that imprisons us, and about how philosophical reflection might help us step out of it. It is now time to start translating these ideas into concrete, practical terms.

The starting point of the philosophical process is always the realization that I am a prisoner of my limitations. Only if I realize how constricted my life is, only if I recognize the narrow boundaries of my world can I start struggling to overcome them. Only if I understand that I am imprisoned in my Platonic cave, can I try to step outside it and enlarge my life.

But what exactly is a Platonic cave?

The perimeter

In everyday life we constantly rely on the way we understand our world—on the way we understand the people around us, on the way we understand the situations in which we find ourselves, on our understanding of who we are, and indeed of life in general. It is only because we understand the situation in a certain way that we feel satisfied or upset, that we react anxiously or hopefully, that we adopt this opinion or that opinion. If, for example, I feel afraid of driving on icy roads, it is because I understand such driving to be risky. If I am angry at my neighbor, it is because I understand her behavior to be unfair or aggressive. Similarly, unless I understand that I am in a supermarket and that a supermarket is where one buys food, I am unable to behave in a way that is appropriate to the situation. I cannot function and feel appropriately without a complex array of understandings of my environment. Although I don't need to think about these matters in a conscious way, I must somehow understand them.

Some of my understandings are about specific facts: about my particular family and neighborhood, about my car or my house. Other understandings are a bit more general: about how to behave in a store, or how money can be used. But there is a special type of understandings that are more fundamental than all the rest. These are my understandings of the basic principles that are at the foundation of life. They are my personal answers to basic life-issues such as: What is meaningful in life? What is true love? What does it mean to be free? What does it mean to be fair or responsible or guilty? What is truth or beauty?

In our daily life, we constantly encounter these basic questions and respond to them. We do so not just in our abstract thoughts, but mainly through our everyday emotions, thoughts, and behaviors. Our plans, choices, jealousies, angers, hopes, desires—these and many others express our specific way of relating to these issues. For example, if I am a workaholic, then my need to constantly work is a statement about what is important in life, even if I am not aware of it. My workaholic urge says, in effect: Productivity is a most important thing in life. To give another example, when I make a special effort to help a poor person, this behavior expresses my understanding of moral responsibilities, namely that people are responsible for each other—although I might not be able to articulate this understanding in words. Similarly, if I feel deeply offended that my spouse disagrees with my political views, this attitude expresses my idea that loving requires agreeing. Likewise, my choices—to watch a simple comedy or a sophisticated movie, to chat with friends or read a book—express my understanding of what is valuable in life. In this sense, we constantly interpret ourselves and others and construct a personal response to basic life-issues, usually without being fully aware of it.

Lisa and Emma are university students working as waitresses at the same local restaurant. They began working there a couple of months ago and immediately felt comfortable with each other. Soon they were friends and started meeting outside work to have lunch together or take walks along the river. But despite their growing friendship, some tensions are now starting to appear.

"You never tell me anything about yourself," Lisa often complains. "Tell me something!"

"Like what? I've got nothing interesting to tell."

"Like, what you did today, for example. Or what your parents are like."

"Come on, that's boring," Emma would say. And Lisa would find herself doing most of the talking. She would tell Emma in great detail about things she did this morning, or what happened to her yesterday, until Emma would get tired of listening.

Emma doesn't feel that she is trying to hide anything personal from Lisa, she simply finds it an uninteresting topic for conversation. "Let's do something fun together!" she would say. "How about going to buy a scarf? Or let's play ping pong—you told me you used to play it as a kid."

One day Lisa learns from a casual remark that Emma and her boyfriend broke up two weeks ago. Lisa is deeply hurt that Emma had told her nothing about it.

"You say I am your my best friend," she exclaims painfully, "but you don't share anything with me. How can you be my friend if you don't bother telling me about things that happen to you?"

When we reflect on the attitudes of these two young women, we can see that they have different understandings of what friendship means—we might even say different "theories" of friendship. For Lisa, friendship means sharing worlds: sharing smaller and bigger details of daily life, joys and pains, concerns and hope. For Emma, in contrast, friendship means doing enjoyable things together. To put it differently, according to Lisa's "theory" of friendship, the "glue" that binds friends together is mutual sharing, while according to Emma's this glue is fun. Interestingly, neither of the two has ever articulated in words what friendship means to them. If we asked them to define friendship, neither of them would know what to say. And yet, their emotions, expectations, and behaviors express a definite understanding of friendship.

Like Lisa and Emma, we constantly interpret our world, and we do so automatically and thoughtlessly. These interpretations are useful—you must interpret your world if you want to live in it, and you'd better do so without taking too much time to think, or else you would never start doing what you should do. But often they are also our prison because they represent a one-sided, narrow, superficial perspective. This comfortable-yet-constricted world can be called our *perimeter.*

My *perimeter* is the world as I normally relate to it, or more accurately as I understand it. It is my way of interpreting my world, portraying certain things as interesting while others as boring, certain goals as worthwhile while others unimportant, certain actions as right while others wrong, certain styles as beautiful while others as ugly. It is, in short, the sum total of my understandings of life, those understandings that are expressed not mainly through my declared opinions, but rather through my habitual behaviors, emotions, and attitudes.

The expression "perimeter" indicates the dual nature of my world. On the one hand, it implies comfort, convenience, and security. A perimeter means the demarcated area around me, my comfort zone, the familiar habitat where I know my way about. On the other hand, the word also indicates an enclosure, a boundary, a limitation. My perimeter determines the kind of meanings that a given action can have in my world, and the kinds of value that a given thing can or cannot have. It also determines the kinds of events that tend to happen in my world (intrigues and conspiracies, for instance, if I am a suspicious person), and the roles I might play (the clown, for example, if I like attracting attention). It determines that some situations are likely to occur in my life over and over again (conflicts, for example, if I interpret the world as a battlefield), and that others are less likely, or are even extremely unlikely. And it is relatively rigid throughout life; it does not change easily. My perimeter marks the boundary of what can be found in my world and what cannot be found there. It is, as Plato would say, my cave.

This is, of course, a simplification. A perimeter is not a simple, sharp line. It is often complex, with many areas of vagueness, gradations, and ambiguity. But putting aside these complications, we may say that a perimeter marks the repertoire of my habitual attitudes towards my world—my usual way of experiencing things, my characteristic reactions and behaviors, emotions, and preferences. It outlines the realm of my possibilities: the type of relationships I might have with others, the kinds of things I might do and say, the activities I might find interesting or pleasurable or frightening, the meaning I could find in love or in God or in freedom. It is the general boundaries of my world.

Where does my perimeter come from? One might hypothesize that some of it originates from my particular upbringing, education, or even genes. Other aspects may originate from the influence of my culture on my way of thinking and feeling. Still other aspects may come from general psychological or biological tendencies shared by all humans. Generally speaking, we might conjecture that a person's perimeter is the result of various psychological mechanisms and processes within and outside him. But the nature of these mechanisms and processes should not interest us here. This is not an issue for philosophy, but for psychology, sociology, anthropology, neuroscience, or in short science. As philosophers, what interests us here is the observation that people are normally enclosed in their perimeter, not the mechanisms behind this fact. My perimeter—regardless of the processes that have produced

it—limits my life to a narrow slice of possibilities, to a tiny
region within the vast horizons of human reality.

*Jason is at a party. He leans against the wall, looking at
the people around him who chat and laugh and flirt with
each other. He feels so different from these cheerful people,
and so superior to them. Whenever somebody talks to him,
he mumbles awkwardly. His words come out too
intellectual, too somber.*

*He scoffs at those silly people who talk loudly and
stupidly as if there was nothing better to do, nothing more
important to talk about. He is not like them, he says to
himself, he is a serious man. He stands erect and immobile,
watching them silently. An invisible wall separates him
from the others—and separates his way of being from other
possible ways of being which are beyond his horizons,
beyond his perimeter. His repertoire is limited to an
intellectual attitude to life.*

*There is nothing wrong with being intellectual
occasionally. But with Jason, this is not a choice. It is the only
way he knows to relate to others, and indeed to life in
general. His intellectual attitude is saying, in effect: "Every
situation and every issue deserves a serious intellectual
attitude." One might say that this is Jason's "theory" of life,
his basic understanding of the proper way to live. And Jason
is following this understanding automatically and
unthinkingly.*

*Interestingly, occasionally Jason dislikes his own
attitude, and he secretly wishes he could be more "easy-
going" as he calls it. But these fleeting dissatisfactions and
longings remain vague at the periphery of his awareness,
and they don't influence his actual behavior. In a later
chapter we will see the importance of these divergent
"voices"—but for now we will only notice that they seem
powerless to make a real difference.*

*This is, then, Jason's cave, or perimeter: He is
imprisoned in the understanding that thinking seriously
and intellectually is the only way to be, whereas
lighthearted behaviors and spontaneous emotions are*

inferior and must be avoided. To be sure, he is not fully aware of this understanding and probably cannot articulate it in words, and yet it influences him profoundly. It controls him to such an extent that he doesn't know how to get rid of it.

A psychologist might wonder about the psychological origins of Jason's attitude: Is it a result of certain childhood experiences? Or a repressed trauma? A consequence of an overly strict education? Or some other psychological cause? But for us as philosophers, this is not the important issue. What is important is not the origin of Jason's understanding, but the fact that he has it now. Regardless of why and where he got it, regardless of the psychological mechanisms that have produced it, this understanding is now functioning in Jason's life as a perimeter, and it limits his repertoire of attitudes to life.

The problem with his perimetral understanding is that it does not allow him to expand himself to a greater range of attitudes, and to use additional inner resources. Jason is obviously much more than an intellectual attitude, but he finds himself unable to connect to this "more." The problem is not that his behavior is "non-functional" or "unsatisfying" as some psychologists might say, but that it is limited to a superficial, automatic part of his being. Even if his perimetral behavior was functional and pleasurable— pushing him to achieve great feats resulting in universal fame—his inner life would still be limited to an automatic surface and lacking in fullness. A philosophical counselor would try to help Jason become aware of his perimeter and eventually search for fuller, richer, and freer fountains of life.

As the examples of Jason, Lisa and Emma demonstrate, our everyday attitudes, especially our emotions and behaviors, express our personal answers to basic life-questions such as: What is important in life? What is true friendship? What is true love? What does it mean to be free? What does it mean to be responsible or guilty? and so on. These understandings form the fundamental coordinates of our world, and they give our life its particular shape and direction.

These fundamental understandings permeate our normal day. They belong not only to intellectuals or philosophers but to every living person. They can be found in virtually every daily moment, in our everyday actions, plans, choices, jealousies, angers, hopes, desires. Like the rules of grammar that govern our speech, or like the laws of mechanics that control the movement of our body, they shape us even though we are hardly aware of them. For instance, it is thanks to my understanding of the meaning of love that I develop a certain kind of romantic relationships, and it is because of my understanding of self-respect that I feel offended; and yet I can rarely articulate these understandings in words.

Since these fundamental understandings are about basic life-issues, they are *philosophical*. This is because they deal not just with a specific detail in my world, but with fundamental principles, with the basic concepts that are the building blocks of my world. One might say that we are all philosophers because we all address fundamental philosophical issues, although not in words. And since our responses to these issues are automatic and unexamined, we are all imprisoned, to one extent or another, in our respective philosophical "theory," which is to say in our perimeter.

Just as, according to Plato, philosophy can lead us out of the cave, philosophical practice can help us step out of this common human condition. The vision of philosophical practice is that we don't have to remain in our prison, even though the journey of going beyond it, of stepping out of our Platonic cave, is not quick or simple. Good philosophical practitioners are people who have the experience, the philosophical knowledge and the wisdom to guide this process, and who are personally engaged in it themselves.

The fundamental insight here is that I am much more than my perimeter. Although most of my everyday moments are confined to the bounds of my perimeter, in truth my range of possibilities is much larger. I belong to a greater reality—just as Plato's cave-dwellers belong to a world much greater than their cave. However, it takes a long philosophical process of self-reflection and self-transformation to realize the broader range of my being.

The Perimeter as a Game

A perimeter can be compared to a game we play. Like a game, it is a limited semblance of reality which is restricted to artificial and rigid rules.

Consider a chess game. We toss a coin. "I am white!"

Indeed, in my mind I *am* white. The white plastic figures on the wooden board are not just mine—they are *me*. When I am absorbed in the game, these figures are the focus of my hopes, of my thoughts, of my regrets and my joys. When the battle rages on the board, I am in real suspense and anxiety; and when the black queen takes my white bishop, I feel a real distress. The actions of the white pieces are my own actions: Through them I move, attack, take revenge, triumph, live. Because they are me. For the duration of the game, the sixty-four black and white squares are my world.

When I play a game, I am transported from real life into another reality—into a chessboard, or a set of cards, or a basketball court, or a battle with monsters on a computer screen. I am no longer the man who lives on Pine Street, whose car needs oil change by next week, who works as a teacher or a bus driver, and who has a doctor's appointment tomorrow. These facts have faded away from my active consciousness. They have almost no existence for me.

And yet, in the back of my mind I know that it's only a game and that I have a doctor's appointment tomorrow. In effect, I am split into two parts: One part of me lives the game, while another part is vaguely aware of the wider world. I live in two different realities at once: the game and the real world.

Playing games is a very common human phenomenon, so common that we usually don't realize how amazing it is. It is amazing that I can *be* the white soldiers on the board and forget my normal concerns and identity. It is amazing that I can live two different lives. Different lives—because in each of them I have different intentions and preferences, different hopes, fears, and behaviors. It is as if there are, within me, two sources of motivation, of thought and emotion, of life.

Games are devices that enable me to live a second life, an alternative reality. In this respect, they are similar to movies and novels. Sitting in the movie theater and watching the screen, I hold my breath when the main character is in danger, and I sigh in relief when she is rescued. I identify myself with the protagonist, with her concerns, fears, hopes. And yet, I don't confuse the two realities with each other. I never mistake a character on the movie screen with the person sitting next to me.

A game has profound similarities to the real world. First, it has rules that limit the player's possible behaviors. In chess, for example, you can move your king only one square at a time, and in basketball you are not allowed kick the ball. Correspondingly, in the "real" world, too, our life is governed by rules: the law of gravity, biological limitations, social norms, moral prohibitions. Our life is also limited by our own personality: our tendencies to be talkative, or bashful, thrifty, or defensive. Just as the rules of basketball or of chess limit the range of possible moves in the game, our psychological tendencies, habits, or fears limit the range of our behaviors.

Second, in addition to rules, a game also has a goal—for example, to take the opponent's king, or to insert the basketball into the hoop, or to kill the monster on the computer screen. Similarly, in real life, too, our actions are directed towards various goals, in other words towards specific desired outcomes: success, love, comfort, security, fun, moral virtue, ideals, etc.

In this sense, the games we play correspond to our perimeters. To put it differently, a perimeter is a kind of game. Games are limited realities—just like perimeters—and this is why we find them so fascinating. But of course, they are not reality. Because the game's rules and goal are imaginary, a make-believe. In a basketball game, we behave *as if* it is important to put the basketball inside the hoop, and *as if* the ball cannot be kicked but only touched by hand. After all, outside the game I don't care at all how the ball is handled and where it is placed. These rules and goals don't have a real power over me. I am bound by them only as long as I accept them, only as long as I identify with them and let them determine my behavior.

The amazing power of games comes from our capacity to identify with imaginary rules and imaginary goals as if they were real. We identify ourselves with fictional situations and push reality out of our awareness. This parallels our tendency to limit ourselves to the boundaries of our perimeter. My talkativeness or shyness or helplessness has no basis in reality, except that something within me accepts it as valid. I am bound by such patterns as long as I accept them—or more accurately, as long as my psychological mechanisms follow them.

There are board games and ball-games and card games, but there are also psychological and social games. I may play the game of "I am pretty" or "I am wise," or "The world is against me," or "I am worthless." These are games if I identify with them, if I pretend that they determine who I am. For example, I may let the idea of "I am pretty" control my behavior and speech, my body posture and my choice of clothes. Or, I may adopt an attitude and style of speaking that are in accordance with "I am a sensitive guy." I then impose on myself specific standards (rules, goals) and restrict myself to them. My reality is now narrower, more rigid, and limited to certain patterns. It is, in other words, a perimeter.

There are also intellectual games: I impose on myself specific standards of thinking and believing—"I am an existentialist," "I am a socialist," "I have a refined taste." In this way, I adjust my thoughts to specific patterns. These are my games if I identify them as my reality, if I let them restrict my way of thinking and being, if I imagine that they determine who I am.

More precisely, it is inaccurate to say that it is *I* who let psychological games control my life. After all, I have never made a conscious decision to play them, I simply found myself having them. Furthermore, my "I" is not separate from these games. It does not reside outside them; it does not choose them and handle them from the outside. Rather, to large extent I am the *product* of these games. The person who is I—my personality, my tendencies, preferences, beliefs—is the result of my games rather than the creator of my games.

In short, we might say that when I play a game I am confined to a narrow imaginary reality. And here again, we see that a perimeter is essentially a game.

Games are not necessarily bad. They can be fun. They can also help us achieve certain goals. Social games help stabilize society. But if I fall into my games without awareness, if I lose myself in them for too long, then I don't live my life fully. I then lose touch with the greater scope of human life. I start living the virtual world that is constructed by the demands of society, by my pretense and fantasies, by the effects of childhood traumas. I start becoming, in other words, my perimeter.

We are amazingly "good" at losing ourselves in fictional rules and goals. American children quickly learn the rules of American identity and culture, and Russian children the rules of Russian identity and culture. American fans cheer for their baseball teams, and the Italians cheer for their Italian soccer team. The poor manual worker dreams of becoming a powerful boss in her company, while the university professor dreams of becoming famous among the two hundred academics in her particular field. The emotions of a shy person revolve around his game of shyness, and those of a narcissistic person revolve around her self-centeredness. Our psychology is amazingly good at adjusting our thoughts, our emotions, aspirations, behaviors to a narrow slice of human reality, namely our perimeter.

Nevertheless, we are not totally imprisoned in our games. The chess-player has some vague awareness that he is playing and that his reality is broader than the chess-board. A wealthy woman at a high-society party may dress and act and feel according to social norms, and yet something in the back of her mind may whisper to her that she is merely acting. I am not totally imprisoned in my perimetral game. Even when I am forced to play by the rules of my psychology, I don't have to completely identify myself with them and restrict my existence to them. Even when I find myself controlled by my habits or obsessions or fears, I can realize that my true reality is greater than my perimeter.

Modern psychology has developed methods of helping people become aware of their destructive psychological "games" and modify them to more functional games. But this task, as valuable as it might be, is still limited. Because going beyond a certain psychological game is not yet going beyond all games. Switching from one perimeter to another perimeter, as comfortable and functional as it may be, still means remaining within the bounds of psychological forces, within the realm of Platonic caves.

The goal of stepping beyond the realm of perimetral games—not beyond this or that specific game but beyond all of them—is the task of philosophical practice as I see it. It is a tremendous task. There can hardly be a more ambitious aspiration. And yet, I believe that it is not impossible. Of course, as a human being I cannot be free of all boundaries. But even so, I don't need to identify myself with them. I don't have to limit my awareness to the realm of games. I can be, at least in part, at least at times, in the broader reality as well. By analogy, if I am forced to play a chess game, I can still be aware of the room in which I play and take part in the conversation that takes place around me.

If this is indeed possible, if I can be greater than my perimetral games and get in touch with a broader realm of human reality, then this should be the task of the discourse that addresses the most fundamental issues of life, namely philosophy.

Chapter 4

Patterns and Forces

My perimeter, or Platonic cave, is not easy for me to recognize. Although it shapes much of my life, it does so implicitly. I usually don't notice it, at least not fully, like a facial expression which I am in the habit of making, or like the intonation of my speech. Often my friends notice these habits before I do. In this respect, a perimeter is not like a headache or an itch, because it is not something which I feel immediately and directly.

My perimeter is composed of my understanding of life—my understanding of myself, of my environment, of my relations to others—but as we have already seen, these are my *lived* understandings, not my verbal opinions. I am like a bird that follows the laws of aerodynamics without being able to articulate these laws in words.

This does not mean that my perimetral understandings are "unconscious." To talk about the unconscious is to assume a psychological theory about hidden mechanisms that are somehow stowed in the dark basements of the psyche, and are responsible for my behavior. These theories should not interest us here. Whatever is the psychological explanation of my perimetral understandings, the point is that they are not easily available to my awareness, just as the rules of grammar which I follow in my speech are not easily available to me. My perimeter is something which I need to investigate and discover, not something which I feel directly.

Often, another person, such as a philosophical practitioner, may help me investigate it. Although it is not something I feel, it is not completely hidden from view. It expresses itself in many ways, some more obvious and some more implicit. Like a nocturnal animal that prowls at night when everybody is asleep, it leaves behind its footprints. These footprints can help us reconstruct the perimeter and sketch its outlines.

Patterns

The most important clue about the perimeter is behavioral and emotional *patterns*. When my understanding of life is restricted to a narrow perimeter, then I have a narrow repertoire of emotions and behaviors, so that I follow specific emotional and behavioral patterns. Therefore, if my behaviors and emotions display a fixed pattern, if they do not utilize the entire range of human possibilities, then this is an indication that my attitude to life is restricted, in other words, that my understanding of life is limited to a narrow perimeter. Thus, if you note that I display a behavioral or emotional pattern, this pattern may serve as an indication that I have a characteristic way of relating to my world, in other words, a specific way understanding it. By examining my patterns, you can figure out the perimetral understandings that lie behind them.

What exactly is a pattern? A pattern is a theme that repeats itself over and over again. It means that in a certain kind of situations I tend to display again and again similar behaviors and emotions. A pattern, therefore, implies a fixed structure. It indicates that my behaviors, emotions, and thoughts are not completely free but follow a habitual formula.

The most straightforward kind of pattern is a simple repetition of the same behavior over and over again. An example is a person who uses every opportunity to argue with others. Whenever an issue comes up, she finds himself arguing. Another example is somebody who is especially talkative, or domineering, suspicious, or apologetic. Given the opportunity, he is likely to repeat the same familiar behavior.

But often a pattern is more complicated. It may consist of diverse kinds of emotions, behaviors, and thoughts that are interconnected in complex ways. If for example, Erica has a pattern of avoiding conflicts, this pattern can express itself in more than one way: She may be quick to agree with others, she may also feel herself too stupid to have an opinion of her own, she may dislike political conversations, she may be in the habit of joking to diffuse tension, to be obedient to her boss, to like playing with her friends fun games, and so on. To give another example, if Edward is always late for meetings, if he cracks silly jokes precisely when he is expected to be serious, if he sometimes gets confused and lost and then boasts about it, and if he feels uncomfortable whenever his boss gives him a task to perform, then these diverse behaviors and emotions may be expressions of one common pattern: the pattern of acting irresponsibly like a child. He seems to be spending a lot of energy repeating this pattern, although he may not be aware that this is what he is doing.

Since patterns may be complex, identifying them is an art. It requires perceptiveness, attentiveness, and much experience.

Anybody who knows Andy knows that he likes wearing flashy clothes, and that he enjoys shocking people with outrageous remarks. When asked why he behaves this way, he explains that "civilized" behaviors are boring. But some of his colleagues at work have noted that, contrary to what he says, when he is in charge of a team he is very "civilized" and not at all bored. He gets mischievous only when he is an ordinary group member, not when he is a team leader. It has been also noted that he doesn't like being by himself, and that, as he has confessed, when he finds himself alone, he indulges in fantasies. His favorite fantasy is of himself being a rock star.

On the surface, these preferences, behaviors, feelings and fantasies seem unrelated. But a closer look will suggest that they all revolve around a common theme, in other words, a common pattern: In all of them Andy seeks to capture other people's attention.

Seeking to capture other people's attention is a pattern which spans a variety of behaviors, emotions, and thoughts. Assuming that this is indeed an important pattern in his life (something that needs to be verified carefully), this means that Andy relates to himself and to others in a very specific way, in other words, that he has a particular perimetral understanding of himself in relation to others. Most likely, this is the understanding that "It is very important to be visible," or perhaps even that "I exist only to the extent that I am being seen and acknowledged by others."

This is still a vague formulation of Andy's perimetral understanding, and more details are needed to sharpen it. In the following chapters we will see how this can be done. For now, it is only important to note that he manifests a complex behavioral and emotional pattern, and that this pattern expresses a certain attitude towards—and therefore an understanding of—himself and others. This understanding forms his perimeter, or Platonic cave, and it manifests itself in a range of characteristic behaviors, feelings, fantasies, thoughts.

It is sometimes objected that emotional or behavioral patterns are not a topic for philosophy but for psychology. But this is incorrect. Detecting a pattern is neither philosophical nor psychological—it is simply a matter of observing the facts and noting connections between them. The difference between philosophy and psychology is in *what we do* with the observed pattern, whether we use it to articulate ideas (understandings) and discuss them as ideas about life-issues, or whether we use the pattern to tap into the workings of the person's psychology. The difference is, in other words, in whether we treat the person's ideas as theories about life that need to be discussed philosophically, or as expressions of psychological processes. If for example, we search for the unconscious emotional mechanism that is responsible for Andy's pattern, then we are obviously doing psychology. But alternatively, we may use Andy's pattern to articulate his way of understanding of life, and then to discuss whether this understanding is coherent and tenable. In this second case we are dealing with ideas about life, and therefore are doing philosophy.

To sharpen the difference between the philosophical and psychological perspectives, consider the following example.

Miriam is a university student. She seems sweet and friendly, and yet she doesn't have good friends. Several students had similar impressions of her: When you first meet her, she is charming. Her smiles are enchanting, and her intimate voice makes you feel as if she is totally with you. And indeed, she is glad to listen to you, to help, and to encourage. You then think that she has taken a special interest in you and that you are going to be great friends. But soon a strange thing happens: You discover that it is impossible to get closer to her. She continues to be nice and helpful, but she finds all kinds of excuses to avoid meeting you too often and become too close to you.

Laura, a classmate, has been hurt by Miriam's behavior, and she asks Miriam directly why she avoids her. Miriam feels bad about hurting Laura and apologizes profusely. And for the next few days she tries making up: She sits next to Laura in class, accompanies her to the cafeteria during class break, and is even sweeter than usual. But soon she starts getting bored with Laura. At the end of the week she is avoiding her again.

Another classmate, Amy, reacts to Miriam more aggressively. She confronts her directly, raises her voice and accuses her of betrayal. A polite, indifferent smile appears on Miriam's face. "What a bore," she says to herself. "She isn't worth the trouble," and erases her from her mind.

When we reflect on this story, we may note a common pattern connecting the various episodes: Miriam is a conqueror: She conquers the hearts of people around her. She cares for them, but only as long as they are not too close, because deep relationships do not interest her. And when a conquest is impossible, as in the case of Amy, she loses interest. In short, her pattern seems to be that of a collector of hearts.

In today's popular culture, one might be inclined to wonder about Miriam's childhood experiences or her unconscious motivations. A psychologist might conjecture that she has difficulties in attachment or commitment, that she is afraid of intimacy, or maybe had an unhealthy relationship with her parents. As we have already seen, however, in philosophical practice we are not interested in psychological diagnoses of hidden causes of behavior. We are interested in exploring ideas, or understandings. We do not make conjectures about why Miriam behaves the way she does, but look at the behavior itself and try to see the kind of statement it makes, the kind of understanding it expresses.

A philosophical practitioner would, therefore, avoid diagnosing Miriam's hidden motivations, and instead examine how she interprets the meaning of relations—her "philosophy of relationships" so to speak. He would start by exploring with Miriam her pattern in detail, examine how it is expressed in her everyday life, and then, as we will see later, would seek to uncover the understanding which it expresses. It may turn out, for example, that underlying Miriam's behavior is the "theory" which says: "Relationships are a game of conquest that leaves you free." The philosopher would then reflect with Miriam on the coherence and tenability of this theory, the assumptions it makes, its implications, and the way it portrays life.

Forces

In addition to patterns, a complementary way to detect a perimetral understanding is by noting resistance to change. This is because our Platonic cave is stable and inflexible. Our perimetral understandings—and therefore the patterns that express them—tend to be rigid. Presumably, they are maintained by "stubborn" mechanisms in our human psychology, although the nature of these hidden mechanisms should not concern us here. For example, for a talkative person it is very difficult to stop talking, and a distrustful person finds it almost impossible to rely on others. We may say that those patterns are maintained by an inner *force* that resists change. A philosophical counselor who tries to expose patterns should watch for signs of such a force.

We are usually not aware of this force acting in our own lives because we don't often resist it and instead let it carry us along. But we feel it strongly once we try changing ourselves. We then discover that change is difficult because the pattern "wants" to continue. It offers resistance. We need a special effort and determination in order to overcome it. For instance, Miriam in the above example would need to make a conscious effort to resist the pattern of a conqueror's behavior. She would probably succeed only for a limited period of time and then slide back, at least occasionally, to her old ways.

This is especially true in the case of universal human patterns that are common to most human beings. For example, most of us try, without any special awareness or conscious effort, to be understood by others, to appear consistent and reasonable, and to make a good impression on our acquaintances. We feel uncomfortable or anxious when we diverge from these patterns. Other types of automatic patterns are culture-based. For example, we commonly follow society's rules of politeness unthinkingly and automatically. But forces are no less at work in personal patterns that are peculiar to the individual.

The result is that although we normally feel as if we are free, in truth we are constrained by our patterns. We are imprisoned in our narrow repertoire, but we don't experience our prison because we are content staying there—this is where we feel natural and comfortable, this is our comfort zone. Thus, when a talkative person speaks, and when an argumentative person argues, they don't feel the walls of their prison as long as they don't try escaping from it. Like a river that flows between two banks, they flow in a narrow channel that is easy and yet restricted. It is only when the river tries climbing over its banks—when the prisoner tries leaving the prison—that he realizes that he is in fact confined. Only when we try breaking away from our patterns do we discover how hard this is, and sometimes impossible.

Many kinds of feelings—anxiety, boredom, awkwardness, to name only a few—pressure us to maintain our usual patterns: When we act unreasonably, for example, we feel anxious to correct or explain ourselves. A shy person feels nervous when she decides to speak in public. A self-centered man feels bored in a conversation about others. An insecure woman feels embarrassed when asked to show her artwork. A smoker feels an irresistible temptation when attempting to stop smoking. A suspicious man feels inauthentic and awkward when trying to express trust. A compulsive talker feels a tremendous urge to speak when requested to listen quietly.

Such feelings and urges pressure us to return to our old familiar patterns, and even if we overcome them once, we are likely to continue feeling them while managing to resist them. In this sense, our patterns are real prison-walls. They act as *forces* that pressure us to remain within them. Therefore, for the philosophical practitioner, resistant behavior is a sign that some perimetral pattern—and therefore some perimetral understanding—is at work.

Shortly after Nancy's marriage, she discovers that she never says "no" to her husband Ken. If, for example, Ken suggests: "How about going out tonight to eat with a few friends, Nancy?" she finds it virtually impossible to refuse.

Tony, the couple's good friend who happens to be a philosophical practitioner, and who has noticed her behavioral pattern in the past, comments: "Saying 'no' is hard sometimes, Nancy, isn't it?"

"What do you mean, Tony? I simply decided to come along."

Tony shrugs. "Sure. Like yesterday when Ken suggested going to the swimming pool; and last week when he suggested watching a movie. I saw hesitation on your face, a reluctant smile—and then, to my surprise, I heard you say: 'Alright, I'm coming!'"

He says it good-heartedly, in a non-judgmental way, and she quickly forgets all about it. But the next day she makes a similar observation, and it leaves her with a nagging feeling that he may be right. After some reflection, she realizes that this is also her attitude towards her parents and towards her two best friends.

Strange, she reflects, her husband is so kind and sweet, and her parents never try imposing their will on her, so why should she be so afraid of saying "no"? Besides, there are many people she is not afraid of contradicting—the neighbors, her colleagues at work, even her boss.

Watching Nancy, Tony realizes that her behavioral pattern is based on a certain understanding of what relationships are. She behaves as if something inside her declares: "Love means total agreement"; as if love is a brittle glass which any slight disharmony might shatter. This personal theory of love warns her that a disagreement would mean rupturing the relationship. In fact, this may be part of a broader understanding: "To love means to merge. If you love somebody, the two of you become one person: one opinion, one behavior, one everything." Such an understanding would probably also lead her to take part in Ken's projects whenever possible, and to feel restless when he is out by himself with his friends.

Nancy decides to break away from her pattern. A few days later, when Ken suggests taking a walk in the park, she looks into his eyes and hesitates. She wants to say no, but his loving face melts away her decision. She feels that she can't disappoint him, that she doesn't have the courage.

"I must try harder," she decides when they return from the park together.

The next evening, when her husband suggests watching together a football game on television, she manages to resist her natural tendency to agree. Instead, she forces herself to reply: "No, not tonight, Kenny. Why don't you watch it by yourself?"

Immediately she is flooded with anxiety. She holds her breath and finds herself searching his face to see if he is angry or offended. For the rest of the evening she is overly nice to him as if trying to compensate him. Later that night, when she waits for him to finish watching the game and join her in bed, she feels nervous. *"This nervousness is stupid," she says to herself. "Why shouldn't I let him be by himself for one evening?"* But her reasoning does not soothe her, and her emotions still speak in the language of her old attitude. She can't conquer her anxiety.

For months she struggles against her emotional-behavioral patterns. But although she becomes better at forcing herself to say "no" to her husband from time to time, nevertheless the difficulty remains. She keeps feeling the urge to merge with him, and only through conscious decisions and effort can she resist it. Indeed, deep in her heart her understanding of love remains unchanged.

Exercise

The goal of this exercise is to experience the forces of your patterns by trying to resist them. In order to experience them most vividly, it is best to choose a pattern that is deeply ingrained in most people. If you are like most of us, who don't like making a fool of themselves, you can do as follows:

Go to a store or an office and ask to buy something that is obviously not sold there. For instance, go to a post office and ask for a tuna sandwich, or go to a restaurant and ask to buy a hammer. Even if you don't have the courage to do so, try to go as far as you can. Whether or not you succeed, be aware of your inner resistance: the tension and anxiety, the cringing, the inner struggle, the effort.

You may be tempted to object: "It's not that I can't do it, I simply *choose* not to annoy the poor guys at the counter," or "I don't think it's right to waste their time." These are probably excuses. Most likely you don't have the courage to do so, which is another way of saying that your pattern is too powerful. This is probably the pattern of following social expectations, and it might express the understanding:

"One should behave as expected," or "One should appear reasonable."

You can also do a similar exercise with a personal pattern that is particularly yours. Again, whether or not you succeed, note the inner resistance, the effort, and the struggle.

Chapter 5

Exploring the Perimetral Landscape

As we have seen, transformational philosophers throughout the ages teach us that philosophy can help us out notice our limited and superficial life, and help us go beyond it towards greater horizons of life. This suggests that the philosophical process is made of two stages: first, a philosophical self-investigation that would reveal our perimeter; second, stepping out of this perimeter.

These two stages are different in nature. The first consists mainly of analyzing an *existing* situation, in other words mapping out perimetral structures. The second stage, in contrast, focuses on exploring *potential* horizons that are not yet realized. Whereas the first stage focuses on observation and analysis, the second must employ sources of creativity and inspiration. The first can be compared to the task of a surveyor, the second to the task of a creator, or a creative explorer.

Since the first stage employs observation and analysis, it is based primarily on standard philosophical thinking tools: analyzing, defining, comparing, exposing hidden assumptions, deducing, and the like. In contrast, the second stage is more creative and experimental. It includes finding new ways of understanding, exploring unknown paths, experimenting and fumbling in the dark. As we will see, this requires very different methods and practices.

The two stages need not be completely separate from each other. They may overlap to some extent and take place side by side. For the sake of clarity, however, in this chapter we will focus only on the first stage of the philosophical journey.

Working with patterns in one-on-one counseling

We always start the philosophical process with self-examination. If we wish to step out of our perimetral prison, we must first investigate what our prison is like. Without knowing our limitations, it is hard to overcome them.

Such an investigation is possible with a small number of participants, especially in one-on-one encounters—in other words in philosophical counseling, and to some extent in philosophical self-reflection groups, which are small, intimate, continuous groups. In larger groups it is difficult to explore the personal perimeter of each participant.

In philosophical counseling, we begin by exploring the most obvious aspects of the counselee's perimeter, namely patterns—emotional, behavioral and thought patterns. Typically, the first two or three sessions are devoted almost exclusively to exposing and articulating these patterns, and this process continues, although in a less focused way, in later sessions as well.

But a common temptation arises here. Counselees often come to the philosophical counselor with a specific problem: a difficulty at work, for instance, or marital dissatisfaction. After all, it is when they experience distress that they seek help. In such a situation, the philosophical counselor might be tempted to search for solutions to resolve the counselee's problem.

From the perspective of the present approach, this is a mistake. Philosophical counselors are not marriage therapists and not career counselors. Their task is not to make the perimetral prison more comfortable, but to help develop the wisdom necessary to step beyond them. This must be explained in advance to the counselee in order to avoid false expectations. If a resolution of the problem is urgent, as in the case of acute anxiety, then this is not a task for philosophy, and the counselee should be referred elsewhere.

This does not mean that the philosophical counselor should avoid discussing with counselees their personal predicaments. On the contrary, distress is a good place to start, because it is alive in the counselee's mind, and because it is often related to a deep tension in the counselee's world. It can serve as a door for going deeper, provide that it is treated as a door, not as a problem to solve.

George is a computer programmer. In the first counseling session he complains to his philosophical counselor, Linda, that things aren't going well at work. Linda explains that the counseling she offers does not aim at solving such problems, but rather at working on George's entire attitude to life.

George agrees, and the counseling begins. "Work is no longer fun," he says. "The new boss monitors very closely what everybody is doing. He is demanding, and I don't feel free and natural anymore. I no longer flow with the work. And the worse part of it is that everybody in the office is happy with the new boss. They take the job 'seriously' now. It's a real drag."

"How this make you feel?"

"I feel bored. Before he came, the office was an exciting place. We turned every task into a game, or a competition: Who could solve this computing problem first? (It was, by the way, my own idea, but everybody liked it.) But now, everybody is soooo serious. They don't joke and chat anymore. And they love the new boss because he is 'professional.' It's disgusting."

At this point Linda resists the temptation to search for satisfactory solutions. Her task as a philosophical counselor is not to produce satisfaction, but to advance George on the path of self-understanding, wisdom, and growth.

As a sensitive counselor, Linda notices that George uses a specific vocabulary: "fun," "exciting," "natural," "flow"— versus "bored," "serious," "a drag." This suggests to her the beginning of a theme, or pattern: George seeks fun. For Linda, this observation is a possible starting point for the exploration of George's perimeter.

"George," she says, *"you are telling me that your main difficulty with your new boss is that work is no longer fun. It sounds as if fun is very important to you."*

"Well, in a way," George shrugs. *"I like fun, but that's not the only thing that interests me in life. I'm also a good worker. I like being productive, I like inventing new things, I like people."*

"Let's look at some of the things you like. Take being productive, for example. What do you like about it? Perhaps you could give an example."

"Sure. Several weeks ago, for instance, we were given a project—we had to upgrade the archiving program. The old program was too inefficient, and we got zillions of complaints about it. Three of us, Lucy and Frank and me, worked on it for almost a month. And let me tell you, the experience of solving one problem after another and improving the program step by step was exhilarating. It was like a video game: You search for the bad guy, find him, shoot him down, and then go up to the next level."

"You are telling me," Linda remarks, *"that this experience was nice because it was like a game."*

"I see what you mean. Well... yes, there was an element of suspense, quick pace, lots of adrenaline. But I wasn't just playing. The project was very challenging. I worked very hard for many weeks."

"You seem to be saying, George, that the project wasn't only a game because it was also challenging. But do games and challenges really contradict each other? After all, most games are challenging. A game isn't fun if it's too easy. Would you prefer your tasks at work to be easy?"

George shakes his head. *"I wouldn't enjoy work at all. It would be just tedious. I need the tension and the excitement. And also the thrill of success—you know, when everything finally falls into place and you feel like jumping up and down, like: Yea, we made it!!!"*

"So you turned the project into a game. It could have been boring, but once you turned it into a game it became enjoyable."

"Yes, you are right. It was my way of making this project exciting."

"I find it interesting, George, that excitement and fun are so important to you."

"Isn't that natural? Doesn't everybody like fun?"

"To some extent, yes, but I wonder whether it's as important to others as it is to you. Everybody like sweets, but most people don't like eating them all the time."

"I've got a sweet tooth for fun!" George jokes.

Now that fun has been identified as an important element in George's world, Linda wants to delve into what exactly it means. After all, fun may mean different things in different contexts and for different people. In order to do so, she wants George to compare his own idea of fun to that of other people, because this could help sharpen what is special to his attitude. A comparison could also encourage him to stop taking his own attitude for granted and realize that there are significant alternatives to it.

"Let's look at it this way," she says. "Did your colleagues, too, treat the project as a fun game?"

George reflects. "Probably not. Frank is not that sort of guy. For him, computer programming is like artwork. When he is punching on the keyboard, he sees himself as an artist, a creator, not a player."

"And Lucy?"

"I don't think Lucy really cares about the job itself. She just wants to be a good girl and get good grades from her Daddy-boss."

"So it seems, George, that your attitude is different from theirs. Not everybody is in search of fun. Frank is looking for artistic satisfaction, Lucy for acceptance."

"Yes, you're right. Excitement and fun—that's my personal style at work."

"And maybe not just at work," the counselor suggests. "Maybe outside work, too, you turn things into games to make them fun and interesting. Let's explore this a little further. Let's look, for example, at your relationships with your friends."

After a short conversation, they start seeing that with friends, too, George wants to have fun. He likes joking and playing and watching sports together. He gets easily bored by serious discussions, as well as by mere relaxation.

A pattern is starting to emerge, and they continue delving into it. They reflect on whether it can indeed be characterized as fun-seeking (sometimes our initial impression is mistaken), whether it characterizes additional domains of George's life, how it is manifested in various situations, and the sort of feelings and thoughts it involves. Once George's pattern is exposed, it will be time to move on, and reflect on how this pattern shapes George's everyday world.

Working with perimetral forces

While searching for patterns, the philosophical practitioner also watches for signs of "stubborn" behaviors that kick in automatically, or which the counselee finds difficult to resist. This stubbornness is likely the perimetral force that maintains a behavioral or emotional pattern. Once the stubbornness of a behavior is discovered, it is very likely that a pattern is involved.

Forces, however, are difficult to detect, since we rarely test our ability to resist them. In the above example, George normally goes along with his playfulness and never feels his behavior as a foreign pattern that needs to be avoided. From his perspective, his playfulness flows out of him naturally and spontaneously—he feels it as part of himself and never thinks of going against it. Likewise, Nancy from the previous chapter normally goes along with her yes-saying tendency. Even when she notices that tendency, she feels it as her own natural behavior, not as something imposed on her by an alien force.

For this reason, when a counselor first suggests to counselees that their behavior follows a fixed pattern, some counselees deny it or try to explain it away. Indeed, it is often shocking to realize that your usual behavior is the result of an automatic force of a pattern, and not of your free will.

It follows that when a counselee rejects the counselor's suggestion of a pattern, this may mean that the counselee has a hard time acknowledging the pattern. But not always. The counselee's rejection might be based on good reasons. Only if sufficient evidence exists can the counselor conclude that a pattern is at hand. In such a case, the counselor's gentle perseverance is needed to encourage the counselee to open his mind and re-examine himself in a variety of situations. This should be done with great caution. There is a subtle yet important difference between encouraging a counselee to re-examine himself open-mindedly and imposing on him an alien interpretation.

From perimetral patterns to perimetral understandings

As mentioned before, the first two or three sessions are typically devoted primarily to exposing the counselee's behavioral and emotional patterns. But for the philosophical practitioner, patterns are not interesting in themselves. Patterns are explored only because they are clues to the main thing: the counselee's way of understanding her world, in other words, her perimetral understandings. Perimetral understandings are what the perimeter (or Platonic cave) is made of, in other words, what limits and impoverishes her life. It is this prison which we seek to transcend in the philosophical practice process.

Here we should recall that perimetral understandings (or understandings for short) are not the same as opinions. Unlike opinions which we think consciously and declare in words, perimetral understandings are embedded in our characteristic behaviors and emotions, often without our awareness. In fact, these two may contradict each other. For example, the fun-seeking behavior of George expresses the understanding that fun is valuable, but at the same time he may be declaring in words—sincerely—that fun is not important. To give another example, when I feel ashamed of having broken down in tears, my feeling of shame may express my understanding that: "Showing weakness is dishonorable" even though the opinions I declare in words may be very different. I may think and say that crying is perfectly legitimate, while at the same time feel ashamed of crying. To give a third example, if I constantly try to control my spouse, then this behavior may be an expression of my understanding that: "Loving means possessing"—even though I may think and declare in words that true love is non-possessive.

These simple examples remind us that in order to expose the counselees' perimetral understandings, it is not a good idea to ask them about their opinions. In the case of George, for instance, if we wish to learn about his understanding of what fun means, it would not help much to ask him what he thinks about fun. Such a question would only yield abstract opinions. It is not his opinions that interest us here but his actual attitude towards fun, in other words, the understanding expressed in his behavior and emotions. And in order to expose this understanding, we need to examine his behavioral and emotional patterns. The philosophical practitioner's role is to guide counselees in this process and to help them see how their understandings act as a perimeter—in other words how they limit life within automatic, rigid, superficial boundaries. A successful exploration of perimetral understandings can later help the counselee embark on the second major stage of the philosophical process, that of exploring ways of stepping out of them.

The transition from exploring patterns to exploring perimetral understandings is extremely important in the philosophical process. It is the connecting point between the level of facts ("I am always embarrassed after I cry") and the philosophical level of ideas ("Expressing weakness is dishonorable"), in other words between the level of behaviors or emotions and the level of understandings.

In philosophical counseling, this transition usually starts taking place more or less in the third or fourth counseling session, after central emotional and behavioral patterns begin to emerge in the first couple of sessions. When the counselee begins to realize that a powerful pattern runs through her everyday life, the counselor can suggest that this pattern might express a certain attitude, or understanding that is worth investigating. For several sessions, the exploration of patterns and understandings might take place side by side. In later sessions, the topic of understandings becomes more dominant, although the topic of patterns never disappears completely.

It is only later, sometimes around the sixth or seventh session, that the issue of how to step beyond the prison of perimetral understandings become central. This marks the transition to the next major stage in the counseling—from understanding one's prison to stepping beyond it. This will be discussed later in the book.

Mike is a mysterious young man. He is a car mechanic, and at work he is known to be a kind and dedicated young worker. People like him, but even his friends find it hard to know what he is thinking and feeling. When you ask him, "What did you think about that movie?" he might smile and say vaguely, "I didn't fall asleep watching it." When you ask him how he feels, he might say, "All sorts of things." And if you insist he might reply impatiently, "Why? You want to put a label on my feelings?"

He has never had a steady girlfriend. Recently he went out with Sylvia to a movie, but his mixed messages confused her and she couldn't figure out what he wanted. Later, in a rare moment of frankness, he confided to a friend that he "couldn't make up his mind whether or not he liked her"— and immediately regretted his frankness. He usually avoids taking sides in a friendly argument or making a decision, but when he is forced to do so he feels anxious. After making a decision he often feels vulnerable and irritated, but when his friends tell him, "You look upset today, Mike," he gets annoyed.

We can see a repeating theme in Mike's attitudes, in other words, a pattern: He avoids identifying himself with any specific feeling or opinion. He tries to remain vague and ambiguous.

This pattern is sustained by a considerable force. He follows it automatically, without thinking about it. When he is pressured to expose himself, a surge of anxiety or irritation prevents him from doing so. Even when he becomes aware of his irritation, he finds it difficult to resist it. A special effort is needed to overcome his anxiety and reveal his thoughts or feelings.

Mike goes to see Linda, the philosophical counselor, and complains about a sense of isolation. In the first session, the two talk about his behavior towards friends and acquaintances. Linda keeps asking for detailed descriptions of concrete incidents. She is not very interested in Mike's generalizations ("I usually do..." or "I often prefer..."), because generalizations are easily skewed by interpretations and preconceptions. People are not very good at observing themselves and understanding their own attitudes. Therefore, as far as possible she wants to hear what exactly happened at particular moments, without Mike's interpretations of these events.

At the end of the first session, Linda explains to Mike the reason for her questions. She suggests that Mike's typical behaviors and feelings might express the way he understands himself in relation to others. This understanding, she says, is worth examining in greater depth. Although the counseling is not intended to solve his problem and make him feel better, a deep self-examination might help him understand his prison and eventually enable him to try freeing himself from it.

In the next two sessions, it becomes gradually clearer that a prominent pattern characterizes many of Mike's behaviors and feelings: He always tries keeping himself vague and undefined. Once the general outlines of this pattern become clear, the counselor's next task is to take a step in a new direction: to the understanding that underlies this pattern.

At the beginning of the fourth session, Mike comments that he is shocked to see how much effort he invests in trying to hide himself.

"But it's not an effort I'm aware of," he muses. "It's not as if I plan my behavior intentionally. It simply flows out of me, naturally. It's just like my dog: He's got all kinds of tricks to *get what he wants, but he doesn't plan them in advance. They are part of who he is."*

He now describes some of his dog's tricks.

A good counselor knows that patterns do not only happen outside the counseling room; they typically manifest themselves in the counseling session too.

"Look at what you are doing now," Linda remarks. "You are changing the topic from yourself to your dog. Is this another example of hiding?"

Mike shrugs. "Something must have reminded me of him."

"That's not the first time you have changed the topic," Linda gently insists. "Earlier on I asked you about your friends, and after a sentence or two you started describing the plot of a movie you had seen with them."

"Which reminds me," Mike blurts, "the joke about the giant and his three friends..." Mike halts, then smiles shyly.

"See?" Linda smiles too. "It's happening again."

"Well... You are probably right. I changed the topic twice in one minute. So what does it mean? I guess it's a trick I'm using to avoid talking about personal things. Which is obviously part of what you call my 'pattern of keeping myself vague.' Alright, we talked about this for three sessions. I realize that this pattern is in virtually everything I do. But what does it mean?"

"An excellent question, Mike. What do you think?"

"Maybe it's because my parents were always analyzing my behavior. I guess that, as a child, this made me feel nervous, so I developed these tricks to hide my real self."

"Maybe you are right," Linda replies, "but this is an issue for a psychologist, not for us. For us, what is important is not the childhood causes of your pattern, but the fact that this pattern exists. Our question is: What is this pattern saying now?"

"It's just like what I said to a lady who came into the garage this morning: It doesn't matter what broke your windshield, Ma'am, whether a bird or a stone. The fact is it's now broken and needs fixing."

"Exactly, Mike, that's a nice metaphor, but let's not get distracted again. What are you really saying when you prevent everybody from seeing what you feel or think? What is your behavior declaring when you change the topic in order not to explain yourself?"

"I guess," Mike says after some thought, "that my behavior is saying: Don't try defining me because I'm not going to fit into your definitions."

"Interesting. You pre-empt any possible attempt to define you even before they try."

Mike chuckles. "Exactly! My behavior says: I'm not going to give you any information about myself because you might use it to capture me with your words."

"Mmm... To capture you? It sounds as though you have a theory about what others want from you."

"Really? I don't know if like theories."

"I don't mean a theory in words," Linda explains. "I mean a theory you express in your attitude. Your attitude towards others seems to be saying something like: Others want to capture me with their words, so I should keep myself undefined."

"Yes. It's best to remain unknown."

He ponders silently for a long moment, and Linda adds, "So through your behavior you are saying that relationships are a sort of battle."

"Relationships are a sort of battle," Mike repeats and nods. "A battle of defining, capturing, hiding. And I am fighting to stay free. I'm a freedom fighter."

"Why is that, Mike? What do you think would happen if others defined you?"

"They'd be putting me in a box, and the next thing you know, they'd be expecting me to do things. And even make me do what they want me to do."

"That's quite a grim view of what people might do to you," suggests Linda.

"I'm not saying everybody is after me. Most people are alright. I like being with people. But I don't like it when they think they know best. So I'm careful."

"This reminds me what you once told me, that you suspected your friends were conspiring to find a girlfriend for you. It also reminds me that when you play chess you always prefer a defensive strategy. If others can manipulate you and hurt you, even out of good will, what does this say about the way you see yourself?"

Mike reflects. "Vulnerable, I guess. Weak."

"And what does this say about the way you see others?"

He snickers. "I know this is absurd. I'm not that weak, and they are not that strong and manipulative. Still, I behave as if they are. But, wait a minute, nobody wants to be hurt by others, right?"

"To some extent—yes, sure. But does everybody work so hard to protect himself the way you do?"

"I guess not," Mike replies pensively. "You know, I don't know where this behavior is coming from. I never realized I am like that."

"Something in you has a certain 'theory' about yourself and others. That theory seems to be saying that the self within you is tender and vulnerable and that the outside world is rough and domineering, even dangerous. This is an interesting theory."

"Wow, I never thought I had theories. But yes, I now realize I've got one. It's saying that it's much safer to hide inside myself than to go outside."

"Which means that your theory makes a sharp distinction between the inside and the outside, the private and the public, the hidden and the visible. I wonder what this 'inside' is supposed to be, what makes it so vulnerable, and how others might threaten it. These are intriguing ideas. It is worth exploring your theory in greater detail."

Intellectually speaking, there is nothing wrong with Mike's theory—one might find reasons for and against it. But when it controls Mike's life, it becomes a prison. Mike is imprisoned in a specific understanding of the self and its relations to others, an understanding that translates itself into a rigid pattern of evasive behavior that is maintained by powerful forces in the form of shyness, irritation, and anxiety. To him, his behavior may seem natural, spontaneous, and probably even free. It is the only attitude he knows, the good old Platonic cave where he has been living for years, and he probably takes it for granted. But once he starts reflecting on himself philosophically, he would realize that he is, in fact, a prisoner of a perimeter.

One might be tempted to hypothesize why Mike behaves the way he does. Is it because of his childhood experience with his parents? Does he hide himself because of low self-esteem? Or is he unconsciously afraid of intimacy? These questions, however, are beside the point here. They are psychological questions because they deal with psychological mechanisms and processes. As such they are of interest to the psychologist, not to the philosopher. What is important in the philosophical journey is the way Mike interprets himself and others, his theory of the world, not the psychological processes in his head.

To see this more clearly, we can compare perimeter investigation to a commentary on a chess game. A chess commentator analyzes the logic of the game: the position of the pieces on the board, the sequence of moves, the strategies and maneuvers, the threats a piece on the board poses and possible defenses against it. The commentator is generally not interested in the psychology of the chess players, in their childhood traumas or their relations with their parents. This is not to deny these psychological factors, only to say that they are not relevant to the meaning of the moves on the chess board.

By analogy, in philosophy we are interested in the logic of Mike's perimeter, in the meaning of his moves, in other words in the network of understandings that compose his world. Philosophy's subject matter is ideas—theories, conceptions, concepts, assumptions—unlike psychology, which studies mechanisms and processes in the person's psyche and environment. The philosophical practitioner would, therefore, focus on Mike's "theory" as a theory, or by analogy, as a chess game.

This is not easy to do nowadays. Contemporary culture is saturated with psychological thinking—in literature, cinema, television talk shows, even in street conversations. We speak almost unthinkingly about "defense mechanisms," "rationalization," "repression," "unconscious desires," in other words about the psychological "cogwheels" of our minds. We are so accustomed to this psychological language that it is often difficult to think about people in a fresh way.

Philosophy speaks in an altogether different language. It is a journey in the realm of fundamental ideas—the person's understandings of life, or philosophy of life— because ideas (or understandings) have the power to shape us.

Exercise

You may have been wondering about your own perimetral understandings. Exploring a perimeter requires much training and experience, just like analyzing a chess game or a work of art. There are no simple tricks, since each perimeter is a unique world, and it expresses itself in a distinctive and complex way. Nevertheless, the following exercise may help you note some aspects of your own perimeter.

For simplicity's sake, let us focus in this exercise on a specific kind of familiar experiences, namely your experiences of discomfort in your interactions with others. This may include, for example, an unsettling encounter with your boss, a sense of irritation with an argumentative friend, or an awkward moment with a stranger in an elevator.

During the next week observe yourself in these situations. Pay special attention to experiences that tend to repeat themselves, such as common thoughts and reactions, emotions, bodily sensations and gestures, or manners of speaking.

When observing yourself, it is important to look at specific moments ("This morning I cringed when Sarah inspected my new shirt") and to avoid generalizations ("Throughout the week I felt uncomfortable with Sarah"). Don't think about what you *usually* did or felt this week, but rather about what you did and felt at specific moments. Particular moments reveal rich and complex details that are not captured by general statements.

At the end of the week, draw on a sheet of paper a circle representing your perimeter. Inside it write the feelings and behaviors that you have observed in yourself. Outside the circle write feelings and behaviors which you found yourself avoiding.

Next, look at your drawing and try to identify at least one pattern that is common to some of the items you have written, in other words, a common theme that appears more than once. For example, imagine that in the course of this exercise you have made the following three observations: (1) When my boss scolded me, I stopped listening. (2) Somebody pushed me when I was standing in line to the cinema, and I ignored her. (3) My friend asked me annoying questions, so I muttered some excuse and walked away. These three items obviously share a common theme, or pattern, namely: "Whenever somebody irritated me, I switched off and turned away (physically or mentally)."

Now that you have found some initial patterns in your everyday behavior, ask yourself what they say about your understanding (or theory) of yourself and of others. What, in other words, do these patterns tell you about the way you understand people around you?

Obviously, this exercise is very preliminary, and the results are likely to be tentative and over-simplified. In reality, patterns and understandings are more complex, and they require much more observation and analysis. Nevertheless, the exercise will give you a taste of what perimeter exploration is like.

Exploring perimetral understandings in philosophical self-reflection groups

So far we have discussed how to explore perimetral understandings in the format of one-on-one philosophical counseling. A similar exploration can take place in a group format as well.

As mentioned earlier, one kind of philosophical group is the *philosophical discussion group*, in which a trained philosophical practitioner offers to the general public a structured activity on specific philosophical topics. Intimacy between participants is limited because the emphasis is on discussing a philosophical topic rather than on the participants' personal lives. Continuity is usually limited too, either because the group meets for only a handful of meetings, or because participants come and go with no commitment to continue participating. As a result, the philosophical discussion group is not a good format for exploring personal perimeters, something that requires continuity, intimacy, and trust.

However, perimeter exploration is possible in another kind of philosophical group, the *philosophical self-reflection group*. This is a closed group in which the participants are committed to attending several sessions, and it emphasizes togetherness and the sharing of personal experiences. As in one-on-one counseling, a self-reflection group can examine the personal experiences of a volunteer, and together reflect on the perimeter which they express. The group as a whole acts as a philosophical counselor, possibly under the guidance of a facilitator who makes sure that the process is done in a respectful and sensitive manner.

But there are also important differences between those two formats. In philosophical counseling there is only one counselee, and it is therefore possible to delve deeply into his perimeter. In contrast, a philosophical self-reflection group consists of several participants, sometimes as many as ten or even fifteen, and it is much more difficult to delve into the perimeter of each participant. Some of the work must be left for participants to do by themselves at home.

Despite this limitation, the advantage of the philosophical self-reflection group is that it can create rich interactions between individuals, enabling them to learn from each other's experiences and to give and receive feedback and support. A good way of utilizing this advantage is to create a shared frame of reference by centering each session on a specific philosophical issue, for example, "What is true love?" or "What does it mean to be free?" or "What is a meaningful moment in life?" The facilitator introduces the selected issue, and can also explain several philosophical approaches to it. The participants then reflect on their personal experiences through those philosophical ideas, using methods such as discussion, role-playing, self-expression through drawing or drama, and contemplative exercises.

For example, if the topic of the session is inner freedom, the companions might start by examining two or three alternative philosophical theories of freedom, and in light of them reflect on their own sense of inner freedom. These philosophical theories are taken not as an authority, but as raw material to develop, modify, or reject as needed. Volunteers share with the group their relevant personal experiences, enabling other participants to witness how other people's perimeters are investigated, to compare themselves to others, to offer support and receive feedback.

Daniel is a member of a philosophical self-reflection group which meets once a week. In the meetings he is very active and helpful. His thoughtful comments help his companions examine themselves, and his empathic attitude encourages them to open up and share their personal experiences.

In their third meeting Irena tells him, "You know, Daniel, you always encourage everybody to speak about themselves, but we still don't know much about you."

Daniel smiles. "Does this make you feel uncomfortable?"

Roger interrupts. "You've just done it again, Daniel! Instead of answering Irena, you threw the question back at her, and avoided talking about yourself."

Daniel realizes that Irena and Roger are right. "Yes, thanks for pointing this out. I guess I avoid exposing myself. An interesting pattern, isn't it? Maybe it's some kind of defense mechanism..."

"Remember," Bruce interrupts him, "we are not doing psychology here. We are doing philosophical practice. The

question is what your pattern tells us about the way you understand yourself and others."

"Would you like the group to discuss this, Daniel?" *Jessica asks.*

Daniel frowns. "I don't know. I'd rather not."

"Why not? What would that make you feel?"

"I guess I'm afraid that my personal life would be the topic of everybody's attention."

"Don't worry, Daniel, you won't be the topic. Our main topic will be the idea of self-exposure. This is, after all, a philosophical group. We need your experiences in order to investigate together what self-exposure means."

"Alright, I agree. Let's make self-exposure the topic of this meeting."

Daniel now tries to explain himself. "I don't like the idea that everybody here would listen to me and talk about me. It would make me feel as if I am a little boy and you are the adults taking care of me."

He also tells them about a recent experience in which he interrupted a conversation with his aunt because she had interrogated him about his life. When the group looks into this experience, it turns out that the aunt was not really "interrogating" him, but probably simply expressing her love and care.

"Don't let anybody look at me personally—that's obviously my pattern," Daniel says. "Something in my head thinks that the personal side of my life is a vulnerable child."

"And it also thinks," Irena adds, "that it's important not to be vulnerable, and not to be a child. I must be a strong, invulnerable big man!"

"What I find interesting here," Bruce says pensively, "is that the distinction between a vulnerable child and a strong adult is so important to you. It's as if it's the most important distinction in life."

Later on, two other companions share their own experiences of self-exposure, and through this comparison they gain some insight into their respective patterns and the understandings expressed through them. Naturally, there is not enough time to go deeply into everyone's perimeter, and the conversation does not go beyond initial insights. But the thoughtful feedback and the supportive atmosphere give them much material to take home with them for further self-reflection.

To sharpen their observations, the group also discusses several philosophical theories of self-exposure. Sartre is mentioned (to be ashamed is to be objectified by another person's look[17]), as well as Nietzsche (with friends "you must not want to see everything"[18]). In this way, the participants develop a network of ideas related to self-exposure, which sheds light on their personal experiences. They realize that life speaks in a variety of ideas that are interrelated in complex ways.

"I'm starting to see my attitude," Heather says, who like Daniel had told the group how she dislikes being at the center of attention. "I don't like it when people talk about me because I hate being passive. I hate being a receiver. I guess my hidden assumption is: If I am a passive receiver, then I stop being 'somebody' anymore. I exist only if I give, help, act."

"An interesting philosophical idea," Melinda says. "To be somebody means to act on others. To receive actions means not to exist."

"Exactly. Didn't the Danish philosopher Kierkegaard discuss the issue of what it means to exist?"

"Yes," Irena says. "He raised a similar question, but in a very different context. Still, it would be interesting to compare your approach to his."

From perimetral understandings to perimetral worldviews

A person normally has several perimetral understandings of different issues: an understanding of what is a meaningful relationship, for instance, an understanding of what is fair and just, an understanding of

---

17. Jean-Paul Sartre, *Being and Nothingness*, New York: Washington Square Press, 1966.

18. *Thus Spoke Zarathustra*, Part 1, "On the Friend," in Walter Kaufmann (ed.), *The Portable Nietzsche*, New York: Penguin Books, 1978, p. 169.

what the self is, and so on. Furthermore, sometimes different situations give rise to different understandings. For example, I may have a suspicious understanding of others when I am among strangers, but a trusting one when I am with my best friends.

Nevertheless, the various understandings that a person has are normally consistent with each other. Rarely do we find somebody who behaves like Dr. Jekyll and Mr. Hyde— like two completely different persons who have two completely different understandings. Even when there is a conflict between one understanding and another, the two tend to be two sides of the same coin. For example, when with strangers I may have an understanding that says: "The other is an unknown danger," while with friends a different understanding that says: "The other is a safe abode." Nevertheless, these may be two sides of the same general understanding: "Friendship is a sanctuary from the dangers of the unknown other."

The result is that the individual's different perimetral understandings typically join together into a coherent overall understanding. This overall understanding can be called a *perimetral worldview*, or in short *worldview*. A *worldview* is, then, the sum total of all the perimetral understandings of a person; or, more accurately, the overall understanding which includes smaller understandings as its parts. A worldview, therefore, is the person's perimeter as a whole.

A worldview is never a random collection of unrelated ideas, but rather a more or less coherent "theory" of the world. Moreover, it usually has a center—a central understanding that is more influential and powerful than others. Other understandings are organized around this center. This makes sense: In everyday life, contradicting understandings create an inner conflict, and therefore they "learn" to adjust themselves to each other.

This does not mean that there is complete harmony between different understandings. Obviously, a worldview often contains tensions and conflicts. But such conflicts are themselves elements within the person's worldview. For example, my worldview may contain the understanding: "On the one hand love is meaningful, but on the other hand love makes you dependent."

My worldview, like the specific understandings of which it is composed, is not something I usually think about in words, but something I live, often without being aware of it. It expresses my overall attitude to myself and my world. Very often it acts as a limited, rigid, automatic constraint on my life, and in this case my worldview is my prison, my Platonic cave, my perimeter. Most people are indeed imprisoned in their perimetral worldview.

Alicia loves to read, especially books she finds deep and wise. She spends hours reading classical literature, poetry, and philosophy, and these books make her feel moved and inspired. On the other hand, she is bored with "trivial" matters—news, popular bestsellers, comedies, small talk. She finds it virtually impossible to engage in them.

Alicia says that she likes people, but in fact she finds it difficult to maintain relations with them. She seems to arouse opposition in others, who often find her cold, unemotional and argumentative. She attributes this to her sincerity and her inability to play social games. But her habits of speaking in great abstractions, of correcting others in conversation, and insisting on her own views, contribute to the sense of distance that she arouses in others. "I have a lot of love in my heart," she says, "but people are not ready to receive it." This, however, does not concern her too much. She enjoys her love as if it was a personal treasure within her. She is not worried about people's tendency to keep a distance from her. She likes being by herself.

Alicia also says that in the company of others she is very timid. In social events she seems shy, and she does not know what she is expected to say. "Socializing is boring," she says, "and I avoid it as much as I can." When she does find herself in a group, she prefers to remain silent.

Now, if we examine these facts about Alicia, they seem to contain at least three different behavioral and emotional patterns: Her interest in deep books and ideas, her cold and argumentative attitude towards others, and her timidity. These seem to express three main perimetral understandings: The understanding that depth is important, that the way to connect to other people is through ideas, and that people are incomprehensible and boring.

However, a closer look would reveal that these are three aspects of one overarching understanding, in other words, one perimetral worldview. Common to the three is the distinction between that which is meaningful and interesting and that which is meaningless and trivial, and it corresponds to the distinction between her private world and the outer social world. According to her worldview, only deep matters deserve attention, and these are located in her private world, which contains the activities that she likes doing by herself: reading, thinking, and feeling love. In other words, her private world is presumably the source of all meaning and depth, the place of the treasures she feels called to nurture and develop. In contrast, the social world, outside her private world, is made of people, conversations, and events that have little meaning or importance. It contains social games, small talk, and similar unworthy matters. A good example is the love she feels towards others: What matters to her is that she feels it in her heart; it is much less important whether or not that love reaches others.

In short, Alice's three understandings are aspects of one single worldview that revolves around one basic idea: Only deep matters that reside within my private world are meaningful and worth nurturing.

In philosophical counseling we usually start by identifying one pattern and then figure out the perimetral understanding that stands behind it. But it is important to remember that this understanding may turn out to be only one small element in a larger worldview which may contain other understandings as well. In order to discover additional understandings, the counselor can direct the conversation towards different topics, different experiences, and different aspects of the person's life. For example, a philosophical conversation might start with the counselee's feeling of boredom at work. After the basic picture starts to become clear, the counselor might ask the counselee about her hobbies, her family relationships, or her friends. It often happens that what at first appears a central understanding turns out to be only an element in a larger worldview.

Exercise
Imagine that in the process of philosophical counseling with a certain counselee, the following three understandings are exposed and articulated:

Understanding 1: Fun is valuable. (An example in the counselee's own words: "I love funny movies. I like to laugh and fool around. I am quite proud of my sense of humor.")
Understanding 2: It is important to be acknowledged. (For example, "Sometimes I get irritated with people, especially when they ignore me or don't understand me.")
Understanding 3: The presence of another person means expectations. ("I am quite nervous when I am in the company of others. I feel they expect of me something, I am not sure what.")

Now, try to imagine several ways in which these three understandings might join together as elements in a larger perimetral worldview. Try summarizing the essence of that worldview in terms of one basic idea.

Chapter 6

Probing the Deeper Meaning of the Perimeter

In the previous chapter we saw that a person's behaviors, emotions, and thoughts are not a random heap of unrelated items, but rather constitute a more or less coherent attitude to life. They express a body of perimetral understandings about various topics, which, taken together, constitute the person's perimetral worldview. We also analyzed a number of concrete case studies of counselees' perimetral understanding and articulated them briefly, in a sentence or two.

This is, in fact, an over-simplification. A perimetral understanding is much more complex than a one-sentence idea. A person's attitude to life cannot be exhausted by a simple formula since it deals with a wide variety of conditions. For example, my perimetral understanding of interpersonal relationships includes my understanding of friends, neighbors, family members, acquaintances and strangers, and each of these relationships may vary depending on my particular tendencies and circumstances. Unless I am a simple automaton, my understanding of relationships must include a network of ideas amounting to an entire theory about what relationships are. Therefore, if we wish to articulate a person's perimetral worldview and the understandings of which it is composed, we must go beyond simple summaries and learn to attend to the finer details. In this chapter we will examine how this can be done.

A perimetral understanding as a philosophical theory

A perimetral understanding can be seen as a theory about a given topic—a theory of love, for example, or of freedom, of meaning, etc.—which explains or interprets everyday instances of that topic. In this respect it is similar to theories that are found in academic books—to a biological theory that explains how photosynthesis works, or to a geological theory that explains how continents are formed, to a psychological theory that explains the effects of traumas, or to a philosophical theory that explains what counts as a moral behavior.

Scientific theories rely largely on empirical findings observed in controlled experiments and observations, and often also on mathematical calculations. A philosophical theory, in contrast, is primarily about fundamental ideas, and it relies mainly on reasoning (whether logical, intuitive, etc.). It is largely a product of thought, and very little of empirical observations. A perimetral understanding, too, deals with fundamental ideas, and it is therefore similar to philosophical theories, like those we might find in philosophy books: Aristotle's theory of friendship, for example, Jean-Jacques Rousseau's theory of authenticity, John Stuart Mill's theory of moral action, or Ortega y Gasset's theory of love. Each of these philosophical theories posits a few basic ideas—concepts, distinctions, assumptions, etc.—and uses them as building blocks to understand the topic at issue.

A theory can be seen as a network of ideas that attempts to shed light on a given subject matter. And this is also the case with a person's perimetral understandings. Of course, the perimetral understandings of the person in the street is not as sophisticated as the philosophical theories of great thinkers. They may be simplistic, distorted, biased, based on faulty reasoning—and yet they are theories, similar in kind though probably not in sophistication, to those we find in philosophy books. In this sense, we might say that every thinking person is a philosopher, although not necessarily a good philosopher. Like a professional philosopher, every thinking individual relates to the world through theories about topics such as love, friendship, morality, or the meaning of life.

It follows that exploring a person's perimetral understandings, or perimetral worldview as a whole, means clarifying the theory that is implicit in that person's everyday life. This is not a simple task. A perimetral understanding is typically not articulated in words but is embedded in everyday behavior. The person herself is usually not aware of the "theory" she lives. The task of clarifying a worldview and describing it in words is, therefore, a work of deciphering.

Furthermore, articulating a philosophical theory in words is a difficult task, certainly for somebody not trained in philosophical thinking. It is difficult to analyze a person's attitudes in terms of abstract ideas. Fortunately, many thinkers throughout the ages have grappled with the main life-issues which human beings face, and have formulated a treasure of insights and theories about them. Philosophical practitioners can, therefore, avail themselves to theories from the history of philosophy.

This does not mean, of course, that a philosophical counselor should impose on the counselee a ready-made philosophical theory. People are different from each other, their understandings are personal, and they don't fit exactly into a theory of Sartre or Buber. Nevertheless, philosophical theories can serve as raw materials to work with, as sources of useful ideas. We can formulate and sharpen our observations by reflecting on the ideas of deep thinkers, adopting some of them, modifying others, rejecting still others. Even when we reject a philosophical theory as completely inapplicable to our counselee, it can still help us articulate the counselee's perimetral understanding by way of contrast.

A case study: Theories of the Other

Donna is not a philosopher, but like everybody else she has her own way of understanding people around her. This understanding shapes her behavior, expectations, hopes, and emotions, even though she is only vaguely aware of it.

It is part of the perimetral worldview in which she is enclosed.

"I am lonely," Donna says to Linda, her philosophical counselor. "I like being by myself, otherwise I lose touch with myself. Still, I wish I had a good friend, someone I could really trust. I'm already 35 years old, and I'm still hoping to find somebody to share my feelings with. But I've experienced too many disappointments."

Donna has an early childhood memory of her grandfather, from the time she was about four years old. She remembers it very clearly: Her grandfather losing his temper and yelling at her. How strange that Donna should remember this particular incident. Her grandfather had always been very loving with her, never raising his voice. That was the only time he lost his temper.

Donna once had a long-term romantic relationship with a man. He was shy and quiet, and for two years they got along very well. And then, six years ago, he was killed in a car accident. This was a very difficult time for her. She felt abandoned by him. In fact, she felt angry at him for leaving her. Rationally she knew that her anger made no sense, but she nevertheless felt it quite intensely for many weeks.

Fortunately, several months later she met another solitary woman, Peggy. The two lonely women became friends. But then Peggy found a boyfriend. "She would disappear for three-four days," Donna tells Linda bitterly, "until I finally understood that she no longer cared about me. So I learned not to expect anything from her."

Eventually, Donna opened a dog-training school. "Animals are easier to get along with," she explains, "especially dogs. They never surprise you. If you are friendly with them, they are loyal to you. People, on the other hand, are too unpredictable."

Indeed, whenever she sees somebody mistreating or mishandling a dog, she can barely control herself. Not long ago she saw in her neighborhood a young woman dragging her dog behind her as if it was a suitcase. Donna exploded. Luckily, a neighbor stopped her from beating up the dog owner.

"This woman is a monster," she said to the neighbor.
The neighbor looked skeptical. "Maybe she was simply
in a bad mood or in a hurry. Or maybe she simply doesn't
know how to relate to dogs."
"No, she is a monster," Donna replied. "And if not a
monster, then she is mentally disturbed."
Interestingly, as critical as Donna is towards others, she
seems to be very forgiving towards herself. When she was
still friendly with Peggy, she would occasionally evade her,
inventing all kinds of excuses not to see her, and yet she did
not feel she was behaving inappropriately.
"It seems," Linda comments, "that you don't demand of
yourself the same loyalty you demand of others."
Donna agrees reluctantly.

Even from this sketchy description, we can start
identifying a central pattern in Donna's relation to other
people: She doesn't trust them. When they befriend her, she
is preoccupied with the possibility that they would
eventually disappoint or abandon her. She tends to have a
one-sided perspective on people's behavior, to amplify to
unrealistic proportions any hint of carelessness, and
interpret it as evidence for their betrayal or cold-
heartedness. Thus, dragging a dog turns into a monstrous
abuse; the death of her boyfriend becomes betrayal; what
she remembers of her grandfather is his rare harshness, not
the many sweet moments they shared together.

Donna's pattern expresses her way of understanding
other people, her "theory" of the meaning of the Other. She
herself has never put her "theory" in words, even though
her behavior expresses it virtually every day. For this
reason, Linda does not ask her for her opinions about the
Other, as inexperienced philosophical counselors tend to
do. She is looking for the understanding that guides her
actual behavior, not for her detached opinions.

A useful way to sharpen Donna's "theory" of the Other is
to read relevant philosophical texts and use them as raw
materials for self-reflection. What is special about good
philosophers is not that their theories are true for

everybody, but that they are capable of putting human experience into words insightfully. They can express their own worldview with great sensitivity, with illuminating observations and concepts, with profound analyses. And yet, their philosophy expresses no more than their own understanding, not Donna's.

Nevertheless, these theories are not without value for her. They can be of great help in mapping out her perimeter, and eventually in preparing her to step beyond it. For this reason, from time to time Linda mentions a relevant philosophical theory, sometimes with the help of a brief text which they read together. The first philosopher she presents to her is Sartre.

Jean-Paul Sartre – the objectifying look[19]

In his book *Being and Nothingness*, the French existentialist Jean-Paul Sartre (1905-1980) describes how the Other appears in my world:

I am in a public park. Not far away there is a lawn and along the edge of that lawn there are benches. Suddenly a man passes by. What do I mean when I assert that this object is *a person*? What is the difference between seeing a bench and seeing a person?

A bench is an object within my world, but a person is more than that. As opposed to a bench, the person over there can see, hear, touch. He has a perspective. The world is seen from his eyes too, and from his perspective the world surrounds him. Furthermore, once the other person enters my world, the objects I see around me—the tree, the bench, the lawn—no longer stand only around me. They are no longer *my* world. They are *his* world too.

This means that once the other person appears, the coordinates of my world are shattered. I am no longer the center of the world because he is a center too. The other person robs the world from me, so to speak. My world flees towards him.

---

19. Jean-Paul Sartre, *Being and Nothingness*, New York: Washington Square Press, 1966.

Moreover, imagine that the man now looks at me. I realize that I am seen by him. I am an object of his look. If I was doing a vulgar movement, I now try to conceal it from his eyes. If I was talking to myself, I now quickly start humming to hide my act. Because I experience myself as the object of his look.

The Other raises a new threat: that I would become a mere object, that I would no longer be a free subject who has a world but a mere object in his world. And of course, he is similarly threatened by my look.

Donna does not seem to like Sartre's theory. "I don't connect to the idea that I am an object for others."

Linda asks her not to judge the theory right away, but to first reflect on it. What is important, she explains, is not so much whether or not Donna likes this theory, but whether she can use elements from it to clarify her own understanding of the Other.

And indeed, with the help of Linda, Donna discovers that she can borrow from Sartre an interesting insight: That encountering an Other means encountering a perspective that is different from hers. The Other inserts into her world a foreign viewpoint consisting of foreign values and preferences. The other therefore means a foreign invader that threatens to change her world.

However, as Linda emphasizes, Donna has no reason to accept Sartre's theory in its entirety. First, several aspects of Sartre's theory are different from hers: She is not afraid that others would objectify her. Sartre's objectifying look is not part of the landscape of her own perimeter. Besides, unlike him, she believes that togetherness is a real possibility.

Second, adopting Sartre's theory would mean entering another Platonic cave, another limited understanding. It would mean replacing her perimeter with another perimeter, another theory, another prison. But she does not need another perimeter. She wants to use philosophical insights to free herself, not to limit herself.

On another occasion, in a later session, the opportunity arises for the counselor to introduce a second philosophical theory about the Other.

José Ortega y Gasset – the hidden inwardness[20]

In his book *Man and People*, the Spanish philosopher José Ortega y Gasset (1883-1955) describes the other person as a surprise. I suddenly discover that I am not the only inhabitant of the world. Somebody else co-exists with me in "my" world, and I cannot relax anymore as I did before.

Previously, my world was cozy and familiar. It was my home, it was mine. In fact, it was the one and only world in existence. But now that the Other has entered my world, there is something unsettling about it: Unlike inanimate objects, the appearance of a person signifies a hidden reality. Behind his eyes there are emotions, thoughts, intentions, and I cannot see what they are. His inwardness is hidden from my view—I can only perceive its external manifestation: his gestures, his facial expressions, the words that come out of his mouth. The other person, therefore, means a hidden source of behavior.

Consequently, the other person is, for me, an unknown. To use Ortega's metaphor, it is as if I was hearing steps in the fog. My reaction would be: "Hey, who goes there?!"

I cannot see his inwardness, but through his body I can see that his inwardness relates to me, that it responds to my presence, just as I can respond to his. In this sense, the other person signifies a danger or a surprise, because I can never fully predict and control the way he would treat me.

But the Other is not only a problem for me. Thanks to his appearance I discover my own boundaries, my limitations, and thus my capacities and incapacities, my tastes, my opinions. Through the other I discover myself.

Donna ponders. Eventually she remarks that Ortega's notion of the Other as a dangerous surprise could shed

---

20. José Ortega y Gasset, *Man and People*, New York: Norton, 1957.

some light on her perimeter. In her perimeter, too, the Other is unpredictable and therefore a potential danger.

But here, so it seems, the similarity ends. In the ensuing conversation with Linda she comes to realize that the rest of Ortega's theory is quite different from her own. For Donna, others are dangerous because they lack good intentions, not only because their inwardness is hidden.

Furthermore, for Ortega I discover myself in my encounters with others, while Donna seems to discover herself in her solitary aloneness. Nevertheless, through the contrast with Ortega's theory Donna manages to sharpen her own attitude.

"Yes, it's true," she admits. "I definitely relate to others as if there is an unknown hidden in their heart; a dormant dark power that may awaken any time and bite me."

Emmanuel Levinas – the other's face[21]

Both Sartre and Ortega present a rather grim picture of the Other. In this respect, they are "relatives" of Dona's attitude towards others. But there are brighter philosophical theories of the Other.

For the French philosopher Emmanuel Levinas (1906-1995), Western philosophy has failed to respect the other person as an Other, as fundamentally different from me, as a reality that is beyond the horizons of my knowledge. Philosophers have always tried to translate the Other into what he calls "the Same"—into my own concepts: They tried to understand women by comparison to men, or non-Western cultures in terms of Western culture. Similarly, they have always understood the Other as just another "I." Levinas regards this as an imperialist attitude because it tries to invade that which is different and make it comprehensible according to my standards.

To truly encounter the Other is to encounter him as radically different. The Other is always beyond my horizons. And this means that his appearance shatters my egocentric

---

21. *Alterity and Transcendence*, New York: Columbia University Press, 1999.

world. When the other enters my world I am no longer free to do whatever I feel like. I now have new responsibilities: I must acknowledge others. The face of the Other expresses the ethical demand: "Do not kill me!"—don't obliterate me.

Note that Levinas' approach does not only offer an analysis of how we relate to others, as do Sartre and Ortega, but also of how we *should* relate to them. It expresses a call, urging us to transcend our normal attitude towards a higher one. However, at this stage we are still dealing with perimeter analysis, and will therefore put aside this call.

Linda helps Donna compare her attitudes to Levinas'. Donna realizes that she can borrow from him the concept of the Other as radically different. But the rest of his picture turns out to be less relevant to her. In contrast to what Levinas suggests, the Other for her is not an ethical demand, but a threatening force. Nevertheless, Donna soon learns something interesting about herself: Levinas' idea of the Other as a moral demand makes her realize that in her own perimeter, too, the Other involves a demand—but in a very different sense. In her perimeter, the demand is on the Other, not on oneself. The Other is, for her, a being who "should" be faithful, caring, and understanding. She, in contrast, has no similar responsibilities towards others.

"I can see it now," Donna muses, "although I don't like what I see. The Other has responsibilities towards me, but I have no responsibilities towards the Other."

"There is quite an asymmetry between you and others," Linda nods.

Later, Donna uses Levinas' ideas to articulate an important reason for this asymmetry: In her perimeter, the Other is not just unpredictable and unknown as Ortega would say, but also completely different from her. Presumably, her own behavior is understandable and rational, while the other person lies beyond the boundaries of rationality and fairness. She sets the moral standards which others should follow.

Martin Buber – *I and You*[22]

In his book *I and Thou*, the Jewish Austrian-born thinker Martin Buber (1878-1965) explains that "I" am not a separate entity. I am defined in terms of my relationships. I am not a separate atom that is independent of others because my relationships are part of who I am.

Buber distinguishes between two kinds of relationships with others (as well as with animals, plants, and even God): I-It and I-You. In relationships of the first type, I treat the other person as an object—an object of perception, an object of knowledge, of manipulation, of care, etc. I look at him, I examine him, I attempt to understand him, I use him. I may do so with good intentions, for example when I try to figure out how to help him, but even so, there is a gap between us: I examine him from a distance, as if he was an object of observation, as something located outside me.

But there is another way of relating to a person: I-You. In this kind of relationship I am *with* the other person. I do not look *at* you from across a distance that separates us, I do not try to know you, to use you, to improve you; I am simply present with you. You are no longer an object in my world, but rather color my entire world with your presence.

In such a situation, I am fully present. Unlike the I-It relationship which involves only a certain part of myself (my thoughts, for example, or a certain feeling), the I-You relationship involves my entire being.

Since my relationships define who I am, I am different when I am in I-You and when I am in I-It. I-It relations are often useful for practical purposes, but I-You is my authentic way of relating. It expresses my full potential, my full being. And although it may last only a few minutes, it gives life to my relationships and therefore to me.

As an example we might think of a marriage which consists only of "correct" behaviors. If the couple does not experience I-You from time to time, then the relationship is dead.

---

22. *I and Thou*, New York: Scribner, 1970.

"You seem to be moved by Buber's words," Linda notes after the two of them read several poetic passages from Buber's book.

"They are beautiful," Donna replies. "The togetherness he talks about is precisely what I long for."

Soon they note, however, that other aspects of Buber's approach are quite foreign to her worldview. Unlike him, she does not define herself in terms of relationships. She is not bothered by distance—in fact, she needs some distance in order to feel in touch with herself. Buber's concepts are not the language of her perimeter.

Nevertheless, through his ideas she discovers that there is a contradiction within her world: On the one hand she longs for I-You relationships, but on the other hand the Other in her world is essentially an object: an object of suspicion, of scrutiny and judgment, of expectations. She now realizes that I-You relationships cannot exist in a world like hers, even though she longs for them. As long as her perimeter does not change, she is not likely to have true I-You relationships.

Mapping out the counselee's perimetral worldview

It is hardly surprising that none of the above four philosophical theories captures exactly Donna's understanding of the Other. A philosophical theory expresses one particular understanding articulated by one particular thinker, and as such it is a single strand in the complex fabric of human attitudes. We cannot expect a real human being to fit into a universal schema.

And yet, as we saw, philosophical theories can be used to shed light on Donna's perimetral worldview even if they are considerably different from it. Her personal attitude is not totally unrelated to that of Sartre or Ortega or Levinas or Buber. Good philosophers are able to describe aspects of human reality in great depth, sensitivity, and detail so that even a partial overlap between their perspective and Donna's can help her map out her understanding.

A useful way to appreciate the structure of a person's perimetral understanding (or the structure of any philosophical theory) is to map out the central ideas of which it is composed. This is because a theory can be seen as a network of ideas. For example, Sartre's understanding of the Other (as well as much of the rest of his philosophy) is a body of ideas which centers on one basic dichotomy: the dichotomy between free consciousness and finished facts or objects, or to use Sartre's terminology, between freedom and facticity. Other important concepts in his philosophy revolve around this central dichotomy. This can be graphically represented in the following "map of ideas":

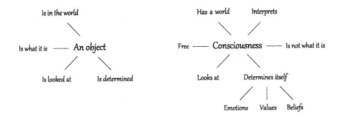

As this map of ideas illustrates, a fundamental tension exists in Sartre's world between me and another person: Each of us can either objectify the other or be objectified by her, in other words, either rob the other of her freedom to interpret her world or be robbed by her and become a fact. True togetherness of two free individuals, therefore, seems impossible. The main concern of an individual living in such a world is maintaining her freedom, refusing to be objectified, and resisting the attempt to be robbed of the world that is hers.

In contrast, the network of ideas that make up Buber's theory of the Other is very different. It has almost no place for Sartre's concepts, such as the objectifying look. Buber's network of ideas revolves around relationships, not individuals. At the center of his theory is the idea that one is determined by one's relationships. This leads to a central dichotomy between I-You and I-It relationships, instead of Sartre's dichotomy of facts versus freedom:

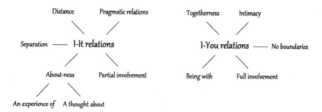

In such a world, the individual's life oscillates between pragmatic relations and intimacy. Clearly, this picture is very different from that of Sartre, even though both deal with the same topic—the Other.

The notion of networks of ideas, and the map which graphically illustrates it can be applied to Ortega and to Levinas, and in fact to every theory about the Other, including Donna's. Donna's understanding to the Other is a philosophical theory just like any other philosophical theory, even though prior to her conversation with Linda she had never put it in words.

In the course of their conversations, Donna explores with her philosophical counselor, Linda, the network of ideas which make up her understanding of the Other. They discover that her world, too, revolves around a central dichotomy, but one that is very different from Sartre or Buber. The basic dichotomy in her world turns out to be not between two kinds of relationships or two modes of being, but between two layers within a person. In Donna's world, a person is understood as a duality of two basic elements: First, the hidden aspect of the person which is composed of dark, self-centered, inconsiderate forces. Second, the visible part of the person which is typically well-behaved and tamed. In a word, the invisible is dark and foreboding, while the visible is mostly well-behaved.

Interestingly, the dark element is identified here as the person's fundamental reality, while the well-behaved element is viewed as a secondary, temporary state, like a momentary island in the midst of a dark abyss. This primordial abyss is transformed into a well-behaved reality only when it comes into view, and it turns back into darkness once it disappears from view.

Since the inwardness of other people is hidden, Donna assumes that it is subject to dark forces. Since her own inwardness is presumably known to her, she views it as fair and reasonable.

On the basis of these reflections, Donna and Linda construct the following map of ideas:

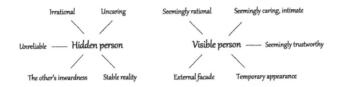

Needless to say, Donna is much more than this sketch—she is a human being, and cannot be squeezed into a simple chart. But this diagram is not intended to capture Donna as a whole. It only sketches some aspects of Donna's perimeter, in other words, some behaviors and attitudes which follow rigid patterns, and as such can be easily defined. Like a geographical map, it cannot possibly encompass every detail of the landscape, only major features of Donna's perimetral worldview, at least approximately.

It is now time for Linda to help Donna examine this map, digest it, compare it to her actual behaviors, and enrich and modify it as necessary. Once they are satisfied that this map delineates Donna's perimeter with reasonable accuracy, it would be time to embark on the second major stage of the philosophical process: finding a way out of the perimeter and stepping out of this prison. This will be discussed in later chapters.

Exploring the perimeter in groups—a case study

Essentially the same process which we have seen in the case of Donna can be applied to group activity, especially self-reflection groups which are long-term, closed groups.

In such a group, delving into the personal worldview of each participant might take too much time, and some private information cannot be discussed in the presence of others. Nevertheless, it is possible to do some perimeter exploration with varying degrees of depth. Various exercises and procedures may be helpful here. For example, the conversation may focus on volunteers who are willing to share their personal experiences, while other participants may help in the questioning process. Or, the participants may be divided into small groups which work in parallel and utilize the time more efficiently.

Linda, the philosopher practitioner, also works with groups. Today is the second meeting of her philosophical self-reflection group, which consists of twelve non-philosophers. The group meets once a week, and each meeting is devoted to a philosophical topic that is personally relevant to at least one participant.

The first meeting was an introductory session. The participants first introduced themselves, and then Linda explained the central topic of the group: the perimetral understandings that shape our everyday experiences. In order to illustrate what a perimeter is, the group examined very briefly several personal experiences which several participants volunteered to share.

Their second meeting is more focused—it is devoted to the topic of duties, in other words, what I ought to do. Linda chose this topic because in the previous meeting two participants, Angela and Phillip, had told the group that they often feel a suffocating sense of duty.

At the beginning of the meeting, Linda asks Angela and Phillip to briefly describe a relevant personal experience. Angela tells the group that in a recent meeting with friends she had a hard time relaxing because she was constantly thinking about what she "ought" to say in order to improve the somewhat confrontational atmosphere. This is quite a common experience with her, she adds. She often tries so hard to be helpful and considerate, that she feels as if she is playing a social game and is not true to herself. Phillip describes how at his workplace he is often driven by a sense of duty, and how he is preoccupied with "the right thing to do." He is concerned that this might make him judgmental, rigid and non-spontaneous.

Linda doesn't want to go more deeply into Angela's and Phillip's intimate life as she normally does in philosophical counseling with an individual counselee. Instead, she invites other participants to react to the two stories and share similar experiences. In the conversation that follows, most of the participants find that they, too, sometimes have similar experiences of "I ought," although of lesser intensities.

"Thank you all for sharing," Linda summarizes the conversation. "Now that we have a collection of similar experiences, let us try to understand them more deeply. Let us try to think what it means to have such an experience."

"For me," Angela starts, "it's like the voice of my conscience telling me what to do."

"I agree," Phillip agrees. "That's what it feels to me too."

"A voice telling me what to do," Linda repeats the words. "That's a very interesting idea. Do you mean, Angela and Phillip, that you feel this voice as something different from yourself? You seem to be saying that there are two persons inside you: one who commands and one who obeys, one who speaks and one who listens and follows."

Angela hesitates. "Well... not exactly. This voice of conscience doesn't feel as part of me. It feels foreign, like somebody else giving me instructions."

"Come on," Jeff object. "It can't be anybody else but you!"

"I'm talking about how this voice feels to me," Angela insists. "I know that in reality it's part of me, but that's not how I experience it. That's what you wanted to know, Linda, right?"

"Exactly. In the philosophical jargon this is called a phenomenological investigation: investigating the experience itself, the way it feels."

"I see," replies Jeff. "In that case, I too have this sort of experience sometimes. It feels like somebody sitting on my

shoulder and judging me and telling me what I'm doing right and what I'm doing wrong."

A few participants nod. They obviously know what he is talking about. But others object that their own personal experiences are quite different.

"Good," Linda replies, "so we have several different kinds of experiences of 'I ought' in this group. Let's try to examine at least some of them today. Let's start with the experience described by Angela and Phillip and some others: a foreign inner voice telling me what I ought to do. Can anybody tell us more about this inner voice? What does it say to you?"

"I think it comes from my parents," Phillip suggests. "When I was a child, they were always strict with me. Maybe I still identify with their voice."

"Freud would agree," Debbie comments. "He calls it the super-ego. You have internalized your parents' judgments."

"Hold on," Linda interrupts. She knows that this is an important opportunity to remind the group of the difference between philosophical thinking and psychological thinking. "Let's remember that we are not doing psychology, and are not interested in psychological conjectures. Psychologists are interested in psychological processes: the processes that make you behave the way you do, the cogwheels of your mind so to speak. In philosophy we are interested in ideas—in our ideas about ourselves and the world. Can we look at Angela's and Phillip's experiences from this perspective?"

"I'm not sure how exactly to do that."

"You are right, Mary. My question is still too vague. Let me explain it with the help of examples. There are several interesting philosophical theories about what we 'ought' to do, in other words about our moral duties. Let's see what they have to say about it."

"You mean that Angela's and Phillip's experiences fit into one of these philosophical theories?"

"Perhaps, Anne, and perhaps not. We will have to check this. Either way, once we understand the language of these *philosophical theories, we will be better equipped to understand the language of our own experiences."*

Linda now starts introducing several moral (ethical[23]) philosophies. "These theories try to tell us, each in its own way, how to make moral decisions, or how to judge whether an action is moral or immoral."

Emmanuel Kant – respect for people's rights[24]

What am I morally obligated to do? The answer given by the important German philosopher Emmanuel Kant (1724-1804) is commonly called "deontological" or "duty-based" ethics. For Kant, my action is morally right if I act with the intention of fulfilling my moral duties. Therefore, what makes my action moral is my intention: A moral action is one which I do not just because I enjoy doing it, not out of self-interest, not even out of pity or empathy or friendship, but out of a sense of obligation. What motivates me to do it is that I realize that it is what I ought to do, that it is my moral duty.

What counts as a moral duty? Kant suggests that there is a general moral law, which he calls the *Categorical Imperative*, that determines all our moral duties. He offers three formulations of this law, which he believes are equivalent to each other.

For our purpose, it would be sufficient to look at one of those formulations. Roughly speaking, the point is that our duty is to treat people (me as well as others) in a way in which rational beings deserve to be treated. Putting it a bit more accurately, we should treat people not only as tools for some purpose but as having an inherent value and worth, as ends in themselves. For example, it would be morally wrong for me to enslave another person, because I would be using her as a tool for my own satisfaction, rather than as a rational being who is responsible for leading her

---

23. I am treating here the words "ethical" and "moral" as synonyms, as is commonly done in the field of ethics.
24. Emmanuel Kant, *Groundwork of the Metaphysics of Morals*, New York: Harper & Row, 1964.

own life. Similarly, it would be wrong for me to lie to somebody because I would be manipulating her without respecting her right to know and decide freely and rationally.

From this perspective, when I face a moral dilemma I should ask myself: How can I fulfill my duty to respect people as autonomous persons, in other words, to treat them as they deserve to be treated—as rational and free individuals who are ends in themselves? How do I behave in a way that would respect their ability to make free and rational decisions? How, in other words, can I respect their responsibility for their actions, their rights over their body and property, and similar rights and responsibilities?

If I keep this question in mind, it would help me decide how to treat people morally. It would help me decide when I have a duty towards somebody and when I don't have such a duty, when to hold a person responsible and when to excuse that person, when I am entitled to do what I want and when I am not.

"I like this theory," Anne exclaims. *"It explains beautifully the experience that Angela and Phillip described: the voice of duty telling them what they ought to do. Both of them are motivated not by their emotions or their desires, but by the voice of duty."*

"True," Phillip agrees. *"My sense of duty is not the same as my feelings and emotions. I sometimes feel like doing one thing, but duty tells me to do something else."*

"A good point," Linda says. *"Is there anything else to add here? What about Kant's idea that it is my duty to respect people as rational individuals who are ends in themselves?"*

"What I experience," Angela ponders, *"is not so much the issue of respect. I'm not thinking about what people deserve, or about their rights and responsibilities. The voice that speaks in me tells me to make sure that everybody feels good, that nobody is distressed."*

"I know what you mean," Debbie joins in. *"When I am with others, I sometimes want to make sure that we are all*

having a good time together, and that there is a sense of togetherness and friendship."

"I think," Linda remarks, *"that I can hear several different voices here, and it is important not to mix them together. The Kantian voice that tells me that it is my duty to respect people as rational beings seems different from the voice that wants to make sure that everybody feels good, and also from the voice that wants us to be friends with each other."*

"They do sound different," David agrees, *"although I can't explain why."*

"Good," says Linda. *"Let's look at a few more philosophical theories and hope that they would help us see those differences."*

John Stuart Mill – as much happiness to as many people as possible[25]

The influential British philosopher John Stuart Mill (1806-1873) offers a different approach to moral behavior and moral dilemmas (which he developed from the philosophy of Jeremy Bentham). He contends that an action is morally right or wrong only if it influences people's happiness or suffering. If the action makes no difference to anybody, if it doesn't change anybody's well-being, then it is neither morally right nor morally wrong. It is neutral.

Therefore, what makes my action right or wrong is its consequences: It is morally right if it gives people more happiness (or reduces more suffering) than alternative actions which I could perform. It is morally wrong if it produces more suffering (or less happiness) than other actions which I could perform. In short, a behavior is morally right if it maximizes happiness.

This means that what is important to Mill is not the intention to follow a duty (as it is for Kant), not respect for people's freedom and rationality, but rather happiness versus suffering. What makes a behavior moral is its influence on people's happiness.

---

25. John Stuart Mill, *Utilitarianism*, Oxford: Oxford University Press, 1998.

It follows that whenever I am in a moral dilemma and am free to choose among several alternative actions, I should ask myself: How shall I act in a way that would add as much happiness to as many people as possible (including me)? For example, I should tell the truth rather than lie whenever the truth is likely to bring people more happiness than the lie. But I should lie when the lie is likely to result in less suffering or more happiness.

Mill called his approach *utilitarianism*, because it tells us to maximize "utility," by which he means people's happiness (or other things that are valuable to them).

An important sub-type of utilitarianism (which perhaps Mill himself believed) should be mentioned here: rule-utilitarianism. Rule-utilitarianism focuses not on the happiness produced by one single action, but on the happiness produced by a general rule of behavior. It focuses, for example, not on the consequences of one particular lie, but on the consequences of lies in general. Accordingly, when I face a moral dilemma I should ask myself: Which general rule of behavior should I follow? And the answer is that I should follow the rule of behavior that has the happiest consequences. This is the rule which, if followed by most people, would bring about more happiness than all other rules.

It follows that I should follow the rule that in general leads to happiness, even if in some special cases it might lead to suffering. For example, even though in some particular cases lying might have happy consequences, lying is immoral because in general it tends to have negative consequences—frustration, hurt, loss of trust, etc. Therefore, I should avoid lying in all cases, as a general rule of behavior.

"This sounds much closer to my own experience," Angela comments. "My own inner voice tells me to make sure that everybody around me is happy."

"Including yourself?" Heather asks. "According to Mill's Utilitarianism, your happiness is important too, no less than

the happiness of any other person. Did I understand it correctly, Linda?"

Linda nods in agreement. "What do you think about it, Angela? Are you a utilitarian?"

"In that case, I guess I am not exactly a utilitarian. Still, I am much closer to utilitarianism than to Kant's deontological theory. For me, just like for Mill, it is important whether people are distressed or content."

"My own opinion," Jeff interjects, "is that although happiness is important, it's not as important as duties. You must do your duty even if it's going to annoy people. So it seems to me that something is missing in Mill's theory."

"That's an interesting issue to explore," Linda replies, "but remember that at the moment we are not discussing which theory is better than others. We are only trying to expose the theory that is hidden in Angela's and in Phillip's experiences. We are not yet evaluating theories, we are only articulating them."

Aristotle – to be a virtuous person[26]

The approach called "Virtue Ethics" was common in ancient Greek philosophy. In modern times it has been revived by several contemporary thinkers. According to this view, our main moral concern should not be *what we do* but rather *who we are*. In other words, our primary moral task in life is not to perform moral *actions*, but rather to be moral *persons*. This naturally raises the question: What counts as a moral person?

Virtue ethicists differ in their answers to this question, but they all agree on the general principle: that a moral person is somebody who has good tendencies and personality traits, or so-called *virtues*. Examples of such a virtue might be courage, honesty, truthfulness, kindness, or generosity. A person who has these virtues is said to be virtuous. To become a moral person you need to develop

---

26. Aristotle, *Nicomachean Ethics*, Cambridge: Cambridge University Press, 2000.

these virtues in yourself. This is obviously a long-term task which might take many years to achieve.

In this respect, virtue ethics is very different both from Kant's deontological approach and from Mill's utilitarianism. The latter two are concerned with what makes an action a moral *action*, while virtue ethics is about moral *personalities*. For virtue ethicists, the basic question I should ask myself is not how I should behave, but rather what kind of a person I should be, in other words: Which personality traits should I maintain and develop?

What happens, then, when a virtue ethicist encounters a moral dilemma and is forced to choose between two behaviors? Should she lie to make her friend feel better, or should she tell the painful truth? Should she give money to a street beggar, or should she not? Unlike the deontologist and the utilitarian, she does not have principles of moral behavior to guide her. How, then, does she resolve such dilemmas?

One answer is that the virtue ethicist has to ask herself how a virtuous person would behave in her place. If for instance, she believes that truthfulness is a virtue and that a virtuous person avoids lying, then she would choose to tell the truth to a friend. Conversely, if she believes that truthfulness is not a virtue, at least not an important one, she might decide to lie to her friend.

Much depends, then, on what exactly a virtuous person is, in other words, which personality traits count as virtues. And here virtue ethicists disagree. Although they all agree that morality is a matter of virtues, they might yet disagree regarding which personality traits these virtues are. Plato, for example, contends in his book *The Republic* that the four main virtues are wisdom, justice, fortitude, and temperance. Others disagree and offer different lists of virtues.

An interesting general approach is given by another ancient Greek philosopher, Aristotle (384-322 BC). According to him, moral virtues are habits which we learn and develop through practice, and which lie between two extremes: between excess and deficiency. Courage, for example, is a virtue because it lies between cowardice and rashness. Similarly, moderation is a virtue because it lies between pleasure-seeking and abstinence. A morally virtuous person is one who has such middle-of-the-road moral traits. Aristotelian ethics tells us, therefore, that we ought to try to become virtuous by developing in ourselves certain personality traits, or moral tendencies, that are not extreme. Doing so would bring us a sense of well-being, or (in Greek) "Eudaimonia."

"Interesting," Anne says, "but this doesn't seem to me what Angela or Phillip have in mind. Their sense of duty tells them how they ought to behave, not what sort of persons they ought to be."

Angela and Phillip agree. "Still," Phillip remarks, "I learned something important from Aristotle: that my own sense of duty speaks in the language of moral actions, not in the language of moral personalities. Thank God," he adds with a smile, "that I am not torturing myself with who I should be, only with what I should do."

There is a moment of silence as the participants ponder. Jeff breaks the silence, speaking hesitantly. "I'm afraid that this is exactly how I am torturing myself sometimes. Very often I am struck by the feeling that I am not a good person, that I should be more patient, more generous, more loving. I realize now that it is a virtue-ethics sort of voice. What does it want from me—to be a saint?"

Several others smile empathically. "I know exactly how you feel," Anne says with a sigh.

Nel Noddings – developing caring relationships[27]

Nel Noddings, a contemporary American philosopher of education, is an important theoretician of so-called "care ethics," which is sometimes considered as a form of feminist ethics. She suggests that traditional ethics—including deontological, utilitarian, and virtue ethics approaches—

---

27. Nel Noddings, *Caring: A Feminine Approach to Ethics and Moral Education*, Berkeley: University of California Press, 1986.

represent a masculine way of thinking. She goes on to identify an alternative feminine way of moral thinking, based on the concept of "care."

Some people have questioned whether care ethics deserves to be regarded as "feminine" and as opposed to traditional approaches that are presumably "masculine." They contend that these approaches are not a matter of gender. We will not try to resolve this debate here. Putting aside the question of feminine versus masculine, the important point is that Noddings distinguishes between two kinds of approaches: justice-based ethics (or morality) and care-based ethics (morality). Justice-based ("masculine") approaches, such as utilitarian and deontological ethics, are focused on the question who is right and who is wrong. They attempt to define general principles that would determine rightness and wrongness. Their main focus is the individual, primarily the individual's rights or happiness.

In contrast, for care ethics (which Noddings regards as feminine) the important thing is the caring relationships between people. Its main issue is not how to respect individuals' rights or improve individuals' happiness, but how to nurture and maintain caring relationships.

From this perspective, when we face an ethical dilemma, our main question should not be: Who is right and who is wrong? but rather: How can I behave in a way that would express and cultivate caring relationships between us?

Although the purpose of the group is not to discuss abstract philosophies, Linda wants to make sure that the participants understand the ideas she has explained, and can see their main implications. For this purpose, the participants discuss for a while the four different ethical theories, apply them to imaginary examples, and compare them to each other. When Linda feels that the group has a general understanding of the material, she stops the discussion and suggests that they now examine how these theories apply to their own personal experiences.

"Hopefully," Linda explains, *"these theories will shed some light on how we experience our voice of conscience. Since our group is too large to talk about the experiences of everyone, let's divide ourselves into four smaller teams. Each team will examine the experiences of one of its members. In this way, we will have four conversations going on in parallel. Phillip and Angela, would you share your personal experiences with your team members? Their role will be to ask you questions and make suggestions to help articulate your voice of conscience and what exactly it is telling you."*

The two agree.

"Does anybody else want to volunteer? We need four volunteers, one for each team."

"I do," says Mark. *"Duty is not something that preoccupies me, but I have my own opinions about what a moral person is obligated to do."*

"Our topic is not opinions, Mark. We are interested in our everyday experiences, in our attitude to life, in our Platonic cave. We want to understand not abstract opinions, but the sense of duty that motivates some of us in everyday life."

Eventually, two more participants volunteer to share their experiences and discuss them with their fellow team members. The participants divide into four teams, each one consisting of one volunteer and two additional members. Each group sits in a different corner of the room.

As a starting point, Linda asks each volunteer to recall a relevant recent experience and to share it with the other team members. The team members are then free to request from the volunteer more details and discuss them among themselves.

Four conversations are now taking place in parallel. Linda walks between them, occasionally stopping to listen to their discussions or to offer comments and suggestions.

Half an hour later, the participants return to the general circle. They share with each other what their team has done and what they have learned about the volunteer's *perimetral understanding. Linda helps them sharpen their observations.*

"Fascinating," Phillip says at the end of the meeting. "I have never noticed that my sense of duty speaks in the language of justice—of right and wrong—at the expense of other important things. I have never realized that there are other legitimate ways to relate to people. I can now see that when I emphasize duty, I downplay the importance of happiness, and of caring relationships. In effect, my sense of duty is declaring: duty is the thing that counts! Forget about what people feel, forget about who these people are, forget about connecting with them—the only thing that matters is whether they are right or wrong."

"That's a courageous observation, Phillip," Linda responds. "We might say that this is part of your perimetral worldview. It is your default way of understanding yourself and others—your automatic theory so to speak. And like any perimeter, it limits your world. Maybe sometime in the future we could think what you might do about it."

Chapter 7

Outside the Perimeter – the Inner Dimension

Now that we are starting to see the structure of the perimeter, we may wonder what it means to step beyond it. To use Plato's terminology, if our cave is our usual understanding of the world, then what does it mean to get out of it? And what might one find out there?

Can philosophical practice aim at the satisfaction of needs?

Earlier I suggested that we should understand the stepping out of the cave as a process of self-transformation. However, the idea of transforming oneself might seem too daunting and even unrealistic. Therefore, it may be tempting to settle for a much more mundane goal and to translate Plato's Allegory of the Cave into familiar, everyday concerns.

Thus, one might think that stepping out of the cave simply means overcoming one's dissatisfaction or distress or dysfunctional behavior, or satisfying whatever personal needs one might have: overcoming shyness and developing assertiveness, improving communication in the family, finding a satisfying career, or controlling one's anxiety.

Such an approach is very common in psychological counseling and psychotherapy, but when applied to philosophy it is fundamentally inadequate, and for a number of reasons. First, this approach distorts and trivializes the great visions of the many transformational philosophers throughout the ages. Instead of questioning our normal life and inspiring us to transcend it, it wants us to go back to normality. Instead of awakening from the "cave" of our small life, it wants to help us embellish our cave and make it more comfortable.

Second, once we give philosophy the task of resolving personal problems and fulfilling needs, we are thereby turning it into a mere tool for achieving satisfaction. This means that philosophical practice is now guided by considerations of the client's well-being, which override philosophical considerations. It no longer matters whether a philosophical process is deep or superficial, coherent or confused, open-minded or dogmatic—as long as it manages to make clients feel better. If for example, as a philosophical practitioner I ask myself whether or not to give the client a certain text to read, or whether to question the client's assumption, my decision should depend on what would promote the client's well-being, not on what would lead to a deeper philosophical understanding. After all, a simple-minded slogan may turn out to better resolve a client's anxiety than a deep philosophical insight. Thus, aiming at clients' satisfaction means betraying philosophy as a search for understanding and wisdom.

Third, once philosophy is given the goal of satisfying needs and promoting satisfaction, it becomes part of the consumerist spirit of contemporary market economy. The philosopher is turned into a supplier of goods that are tailored to fit the client's apparent needs, just like the chef who prepares food in accordance with customers' taste, just like the plastic surgeon who modifies noses to satisfy the need to feel admired, or the interior designer who designs living rooms to satisfy people's need for convenience and elegance. The result is that philosophy, which has always aspired to be a critic of accepted social norms, now becomes just another player *within* society. Instead of radically questioning and examining our perceived needs, it is now turned into a satisfier of such needs. Philosophical practitioners now find themselves adjusting their practice to the demands of the market, to the needs and goals declared by clients. They are no longer a Socrates or a

Rousseau or a Nietzsche who shakes people out of their smug delusions and pursuit of self-satisfaction, who cry out to society what society does not want to hear, but rather are domesticated professionals who seek to satisfy.

Of course, there is nothing wrong with helping people feel better, but this is no longer philosophy in the original sense of philo-sophia, of love of wisdom and search for truth and understanding. Philosophy in its deep sense is a critic of our perceived needs, not a satisfier of needs. Its aim is to arouse discontent, not to offer satisfaction. It seeks to evoke perplexity and wonder, not to produce solutions and complacency; to encourage an appreciation of the complexity and richness of life, not to simplify life into solutions and bottom lines. True philosophical practice seeks to question all that is "normal," not to lead people to normality.

Philosophical practitioners often mention Socrates and Plato as their role-models. But Socrates was certainly not a satisfier of needs; he was a provocateur. To his "counselees" he offered agitation, wonder, confusion, creative dissatisfaction. Similarly, Plato sought to pull people out of their narrow cave, out of their world of shadows—which is to say, out of their "normal" conceptions and perceived needs. His aim was not to solve problems *within* their cave—how to deal with the boss, how to feel better with oneself, how to find a satisfying career—but to arouse in them a dormant yearning to go beyond their cave, beyond their felt concerns.

In this Socratic and Platonic sense, the true philosopher is an agitator, a revolutionary, and for a very good reason: The search for wisdom requires questioning the obvious, forsaking our previous convictions, sacrificing our self-content and security, turning our back to perceived needs and values, and venturing into an uncharted terrain.

A closer look at some transformational thinkers

A better understanding of the meaning of stepping out of the cave can be found in the writings of the transformational philosophers. As I have already said, common to all of them is a distinction between two attitudes to life, one that is limited and one that is fuller. Although this distinction may be a matter of degree rather than a sharp dichotomy, for the sake of simplicity we may focus on the two extreme poles. While in the first attitude we engage only superficial aspects of ourselves, in the fuller attitude we engage deeper aspects of our being.

For a better understanding of what this means, let us examine in greater detail a handful of examples. I chose to focus here on Rousseau, Bergson, Buber, and Marcus Aurelius as a representative sample of the entire group since they are very different from each other and therefore cover a broad scope of possible perspectives. As we will see, despite the differences between them, they are variations on the same common themes.

Jean-Jacques Rousseau – the natural self versus the false mask

Rousseau was an important 18th-century French philosopher whose writings had an immense impact on modern thought. In his book *Emile*[28] he distinguishes between the false, artificial, social self and the natural, true self.

A central concern for Rousseau is the social games people play through which they develop a false sense of self. People follow social norms, they adjust themselves to ways of speaking and behaving that are socially acceptable or respectable, they aspire to own what their neighbors own, and they think and feel in prescribed ways. This is not merely an external behavior that people put on. Worse, people are inculcated into these patterns of thought, emotion, and behavior, so that they come to identify themselves with the social games they play. Their life becomes distant from their own true self, and in this sense they become alienated from themselves.

Several psychological processes are responsible for this alienation, including comparing oneself to others,

---

28. *Emile*, New York: Basic Books, 1979.

succumbing to external pressure, mimicking, manipulating, and acting out of pride and self-love. The result is that the individual develops a false conception of who he is, which is to say, a false self. But since he identifies with this false self, he is not aware of its falseness.

The solution to this alienated human condition, according to Rousseau, is an education that would start from early childhood. It would insulate children from destructive social influences, and as long as they are still young and impressionable would place them in a protective educational setting where their authentic sources of life would be free to develop without external distortion.

Here Rousseau makes an important (and arguable) assumption, namely, that we possess natural inner resources that are quite independent of society's influence. These resources are what he calls the *natural self*. The natural self represents the person's inborn potentials and can be compared to the inborn nature of a tree, which has the potential to develop from a seed into a healthy tree with a healthy trunk, branches, and leaves. In order for this inner nature to work, the tree needs basic conditions such as soil and sun and water so that its inner nature would express itself in full. In a similar way, an authentic person is animated by an inner self—a source of self-motivated energies that are spontaneous, productive, autonomous, self-reliant, and good-hearted—which need some basic conditions in order to express themselves fully in the growing process. Hence, the role which Rousseau envisions for education is to create the "greenhouse" in which the young plant would grow healthily before moving to society. The educator is compared to a gardener who does not attempt to dictate to the young plant how to grow, but only provides the conditions that would allow the natural potentials to unfold optimally.

Rousseau's vision can be criticized as employing a simplistic distinction between social influences and inner resources. One might object that a self that is not shaped by societal influences cannot be a complete and healthy individual. Societal influences are an essential part of growth, maturity, self-understanding, and self-identity.

This is a legitimate objection, but we need not discuss it here. For our purpose, we can regard the details of Rousseau's theory as the external garb of a fundamental vision that inspired him: that the everyday facet of our self is not all that we can be, and is not even the deepest and truest part of ourselves. Our truer and deeper self is usually dormant and ignored, and only under appropriate conditions can be awakened.

Note that Rousseau's false self is a psychological structure that follows specific patterns: the tendency to compare, manipulate, imitate, play power games, etc. It is a psychological *mechanism*, and this is why it expresses itself in fixed patterns.

In contrast, Rousseau's natural self is not governed by psychological mechanisms and does not follow any such patterns. It is, rather, spontaneous and free. Indeed, it is barely describable at all. While Rousseau describes in detail the mechanisms that shape and control our false self, he says very little about the structure of our natural self. What he tells us about Emile—his fictional example of a natural child—is a story, a specific example, not a generalized theory, and certainly not a theory about Emile's psychology. This is understandable. The natural self lacks definable mechanisms and behavioral patterns, and as such it cannot be captured by general formulas.

But how can the natural self shape our behavior, thoughts, and emotions if it is not a psychological mechanism? Although Rousseau does not say so explicitly, I suggest that the natural self belongs to a category that is altogether different from that of the false self. Rousseau's natural self is a fountain of energies and motivations, rather than a mechanism that controls and shapes. The authentic person is nurtured by an inner self and flows from it, rather than being ruled by it.

Thus we see here a dichotomy between two mental realities: One is governed by mechanisms that impose on us behavioral and psychological patterns, while the other flows freely from a fountain of life-energies. This is a dichotomy between a mechanism and a fountain, patterns versus spontaneity, controlling forces versus plenitude.

Henri Bergson – *wholeness versus fragmentation*

A similar distinction is found in the writings of most other transformational thinkers, although each of them looks at it from a different viewpoint. To see another example, let us now leap three centuries forward to Henri Bergson, a French philosopher and Noble Prize laureate who was especially influential at the beginning of the 20th century, but whose influence is still felt in contemporary European philosophy.

Unlike Rousseau, whose interests focus primarily on the relationship between the individual and society, Bergson focuses on our inner mental life and the way it flows through time. In his book *Time and Free Will*[29] he argues that the various elements of our mental life—the many shades of emotions, sensations, feelings, thoughts, images, etc. —are organized in a unique way which is fundamentally different from the organization of material objects. Stones and chairs and houses are fixed and stable "things" that are separate from each other. They have determinate properties, they occupy a specific location in the dimensions of space and time, they are external to each other, and they are made of (or can be broken into) independent, separate parts.

In contrast, our mental life has an organization which Bergson calls "duration": a holistic flow of qualities that interpenetrate each other. These qualities, unlike material objects, are neither separate elements nor stable through time. When I drink a glass of wine, for example, its taste is not completely distinct from the sensation of smell in my nostrils, from the sensation of texture in my mouth, from the pleasure of togetherness I feel with my friends, or even from the headache or anxiety that I happen to have. These

---

29. Henri Bergson, *Time and Free Will*, New York: Dover Publications, 2001.

qualities "color" one another. They are also colored by previous moments—by the food I ate ten minutes ago, or by the irritating conversation I have just had. And since the past constantly grows moment after moment, a mental quality never remains the same over time. The first moment of drinking wine, for instance, is not the same as a moment later, when the sensation of taste has spread from a gentle tingling on the tongue to the entire mouth, and not the same as the taste of the second or third glass, when the sensation is heavy and dull. The past constantly accumulates additional qualities as time goes by, so that every experience constantly changes.

Furthermore, strictly speaking, one cannot even talk about different intensities of the same sensation. The quality of a "weak" headache—say, a sharp pinch in the temple—is not the same as the hammer-like quality of a "strong" headache that reverberates throughout my entire head. Different headaches differ not just in their intensities but in their basic qualities. It is only language that groups them together and portrays them as different intensities of the same thing.

Thus, our inner mental life is not a permutation of fixed qualities that are merely reorganized in different combinations and intensities, but rather an ever-changing, creative, holistic flow of interpenetrating and novel qualities. It is only for the sake of simplification and communication that we treat our mental life as if it was made of separate, stable, and measurable elements with varying intensities. We extract a specific quality from the flow in which it appears, ignore shades and gradual changes, and impose on it clear-cut characterizations: "headache," "love," "greater happiness," "the same anger."

The consequence of these linguistic abstractions is far-reaching. Little by little they become real in our minds because they impose themselves on our mental qualities, which crystallize and turn into separable fragments. A crust forms on the flow of our mental life—a crust made of mental qualities that are no longer alive and flowing, but are distinct and fixed. These lifeless mental items float on the holistic mental flow like dead leaves on a pond. Gradually we come to ignore the rich current that flows deep below them and so we start living mainly on the surface of our being.

As a result, we lose touch with the fullness of our inner life. Most of the time we don't even realize that the life we live is only a crust of crystallized and lifeless mental items, and that these separate items no longer flow in a creative symphony, but rather follow fixed mechanistic patterns. At this level we are not fully ourselves. It is only in special moments that the deeper flow of our mental life breaks through the surface and erupts. It is only then that we express our entire and true being fully and freely.

But although we are usually oblivious to the symphonic flow of our mental life, we have the capacity to notice it. This is what Bergson calls *intuition*. Intuition, for Bergson, is a way of understanding which is holistic and direct. It apprehends the whole without breaking the whole into parts, without imposing on it concepts and distinctions. It is, further, a way of understanding life from the inside, which connects us to the river of life directly.

It is striking how similar Bergson's and Rousseau's theories are despite their obvious differences. They both draw a distinction between two aspects of our inner life: a superficial layer of our life that is produced by structures that are externally imposed versus a deep, authentic, and free inner life that emerges from the fullness of the deep self. For both thinkers, the result is that normally we don't live our everyday life in its potential fullness; that the superficial life we usually live is distorted by foreign structures; that these structures limit life to narrow and artificial ways of relating to ourselves and our world; and that there are greater sources within us which we do not normally recognize and utilize. Evidently, the two thinkers express the same realization, each thinker in terms of his own concepts and ideas.

Martin Buber – togetherness versus distance
For our third case study I chose Martin Buber—an influential 20th-century Austrian-born Israeli philosopher—precisely because his philosophy seems so different from that of either Rousseau or Bergson. We have already encountered him briefly earlier in this book, and it is now time to look at his ideas in greater detail.

Buber locates the authentic life in interpersonal relations to other persons, in contrast to Rousseau's and Bergson's individualistic visions that regard the source of authentic life as lying within the individual. But despite this obvious difference, we can find the same central theme running through Buber's writings, the same basic distinction between two ways of being.

In his book *I and Thou*[30] Buber explains that we usually assume towards others what he calls I-It relations. I stand in an I-It relation to another person when I relate to her as an object—an object of my thoughts, of my emotions, of my experiences, etc. This happen, for example, when I try to figure out what she thinks, or when I analyze or psychologize her, when I form an impression of her or a thought about her, when I look at her with curiosity, treat her as a disturbance or as a means for satisfying my needs, fantasize about her, fear her, manipulate her, etc. I-It relationships need not necessarily involve negative intentions. For example, I may be a benevolent psychologist or a loving friend who wishes to cure the other person's tormented soul. If I try to figure out what worries her or to investigate the source of her distress, I thereby assume an I-It relation towards her.

We can assume I-It relations towards other persons, but also towards nature, plants and animals, works of music and art, and even God. This happens when we treat them as objects of our thoughts or of our experiences, as things to figure out or manipulate or use. Our everyday life is usually dominated by I-It relations.

---

30. *I and Thou*, New York: Scribner's, 1970.

The problem with I-It relations is that they are partial, remote, and alienating. First, since the Other in the I-It relation is an object for me, I relate to her through thoughts or experiences that are *about* her. This about-ness means that we are external to one another. A gulf separates us— the gulf between subject and object, the onlooker and the one looked upon.

Furthermore, only a limited part of me is involved in I-It relations, namely the thoughts or experiences which I employ at the moment. I may, for example, experience interest in the other person while the rest of my personality remains unengaged. Or, I may follow her words with respect and enjoyment, but without involving the rest of me.

Thus, I-It relations are objectifying, distancing, and partial. And since for Buber relationships are at the heart of human existence, this means that when I assume these relations I do not live my life in full.

Here Buber's views parallel the basic insight of Rousseau and Bergson: In everyday life I am usually not true to the potential fullness of my being, although I am normally unaware of this inauthentic condition. Moreover, like the other two thinkers, Buber too suggests that I can overcome this alienated, impoverished state. What is needed is a change that would fundamentally transform, at least temporarily, my way of relating to other people and to the world.

For Buber, such a transformation is only partly within my powers. I can be attentive and open to it, but it also has a life of its own. It sometimes appears for a few moments, as if by itself, and then goes away. This is a transformation to what Buber calls I-You (or I-Thou) relations.

When I stand in an I-You relation to another person, I am *with* her with my entire being. This happens, for example, at special moments when an ineffable togetherness binds me to another person—sometimes a friend but sometimes a total stranger. At those moments I do not think about the other person, I do not guess what she feels. No knowledge or thought or experiencing separates between us, no about-ness relation is needed to bridge the gap between our lives, since no such gap exists. We are bound by togetherness, as a basic relation which cannot be analyzed into smaller elements. At those moments we are fully present in our relation, in our entire totality, and are therefore true to the fullness of our being. Through this I-You relation we attain our authenticity. Although it is impossible to maintain it all the time, it is a source of meaning and value to all interactions and to life in general.

As we can see, Buber, like Rousseau and Bergson, suggests that a self-transformation can bring us in touch with the fullness of our being, that it can enable us to establish a fuller relationship to life, and thus live authentically. But Buber makes here an additional point which is less prominent in the other two approaches. To see this, note that Buber challenges a seemingly obvious assumption, namely, that as a person I am a self-contained entity whose existence is separable from other persons and things around me. According to this common assumption, my nature and identity are independent of others around me, just as a rock is in principle independent from other rocks.

But according to Buber, it is only in the alienated I-It relations that we are such separate, self-contained atoms. In my deeper reality, which appears in the I-Thou mode, my relations to others are part of who I am. I am a person-in-relation, so that my essence includes my relations to other people, to things, to nature, to ideas, to God. In other words, I am fundamentally relational, fundamentally turning beyond myself. The sources of my existence—those that give me life, meaning, identity—are not in me alone, but in my being with others.

We have already seen a seed of a similar idea in Bergson. Bergson maintains that our mental qualities are not separate things that are external to each other because they always interpenetrate neighboring qualities and are open beyond themselves. Buber goes a step further when he suggests that a person as a whole is not a self-enclosed entity. In my fundamental reality, as it is revealed in I-You relations, I am open to the other, and in this sense I am more than myself. In fact, in Bergson's later book, *Creative Evolution*, a person's life is portrayed as part of the overall flow of life on earth.[31]

Marcus Aurelius – taking part in the Cosmos

This last theme—of our fundamental openness to beyond ourselves—has already been developed centuries earlier by Stoicism, an important philosophical school that flourished in the ancient Hellenistic world. An interesting example is found in book *Meditations*[32], written by the second-century Stoic philosopher (and Roman Emperor) Marcus Aurelius.

In a later chapter I will discuss this book in greater detail. For now, suffices it to say that it envisions a self-transformation from psychological slavery to inner rational freedom. For Marcus Aurelius, we are usually controlled by psychological forces such as desires and fears, and in this way betray our true self, which is our capacity to act freely and with reason. When we succumb to our psychological forces, we allow ourselves to be attached to objects of desire, to be discontent with what we have, to be anxious about the future, and to be victims of regret, jealousy, anger and other distressing emotions. This is not only a state of slavery but also of unhappiness.

Reason, in contrast, can set us free from false desires and worries, since it tells us to accept whatever happens to us in tranquility under every possible circumstance. Reason is our essential nature as human beings. It is our "guiding principle" (or "daemon") which resides in each person's soul, but in everyday life we usually forget it and lose touch with it as we immerse ourselves in our daily concerns. It takes special philosophical exercises to awaken within us an awareness of our prison and bring us back to our true self, our guiding principle.

So far we see in Marcus Aurelius similar transformational themes to those of other philosophers.

---

31. *Creative Evolution*, Lanham, MD: University Press of America, 1983.
32. *Meditations*, Amherst: Prometheus Books, 1991.

But an additional idea is worth emphasizing: Reason guides not only human beings but also the universe in general. The universe is a cosmos—a harmonious and organized system that behaves in accordance with the universal Logos, or reason. It is, therefore, a good world, where everything happens as it should. If we are tempted to regard what happens to us as imperfect and lamentable, it is only because we cling to our narrow, self-centered desires and fail to see the larger picture. We expect the world to satisfy our expectations.

Once we let go of our self-centered viewpoint and look at life from the broader perspective of universal reason, we realize that it is a perfect world, indeed a sacred world. This is why Marcus Aurelius reminds himself again and again throughout his book to look at himself in the context of the cosmos, and to remember that he is a minuscule part of this sacred whole. This is not a pessimistic outlook. On the contrary, by understanding that we are tiny details in a vast universe we are set free from our petty concerns and we come to see ourselves as taking part in the greater order of things. Our tiny life receives value and meaning from the whole.

We need not buy into Stoic metaphysics in order to appreciate the fundamental insight that underlies this metaphysics: that we should view ourselves not as isolated atoms, but rather as parts of a larger whole. By adopting a broader perspective we transcend our small personal worldview.

This is, then, the transformation suggested in Marcus Aurelius writings: We ought to overcome our absorptions in ourselves and in our desires and open the boundaries of our self-centered world to the larger horizons of reality. This requires a profound change in our understanding of ourselves, of others, and of our world. It requires us to stop encountering everyday events from the exclusive perspective of our personal interests, as if we were the center of the world, but from the universal perspective.

The inner dimension of depth

The above four thinkers—Rousseau, Bergson, Buber, and Marcus Aurelius—are only a sample of a larger group of transformational thinkers throughout history who envisioned a self-transformation guided by philosophy. From what we have just seen, it is clear that they were inspired by a similar vision, namely, that we usually live a constricted, mechanical, fragmented life which we are nevertheless capable of transcending. Not only *can* we transcend these limitations, but we *ought* to do so. Deep within us there is a yearning—a *call*—to transform ourselves and come to live a greater, fuller, richer life.

The transformations envisioned by these four philosophies are obviously different from each other in important respects, but nevertheless they share several important characteristics:

1. Preciousness: Perhaps the most obvious theme shared by these philosophers is the idea that the transformed state is experienced as having a special value. Normally, many of our everyday moments feel insignificant, barely conscious, dull, forgettable. In contrast, in the transformed state, each moment is experienced as valuable, each moment gives us a sense of special significance—not because it is useful for some future purpose, but because it is significant in itself. A Stoic moment of focused tranquility in harmony with the cosmos, a moment of Rousseau's simple and free spontaneity, a Bergsonian moment of rich symphonic flow, or a Buberian togetherness—each of these is felt as precious, at times even as sacred.

2. Fullness: The preciousness of the moment is partly due to the sense of being fully and directly conscious of reality—the reality of ourselves, of others, of the world. The typical fog of inattention and automaticity is gone, we appreciate the moment in its fullness, and this appreciation is alive in us and intense. This is not a theoretical kind of appreciation—we do not acquire a new theory about previously unknown facts, but we are directly aware of the fullness and richness of reality within and outside us.

3. Self-unity. Normally, when I am ruled by my psychological mechanisms and forces, I am fragmented. Parts of me are activated by different forces and mechanisms expressing incoherent attitudes and understandings. In contrast, in the transformed state I am one. My thoughts, emotions, and behaviors are no longer separate and isolated, no longer pulling in distinct directions, but are part of a unified whole.

Thus, my behavior no longer comes from disparate psychological forces that impose on me their rules and agendas, but it emerges from my inner being. I am moved by one single source—the Stoic Logos, the spontaneous natural self, the Bergsonian flow, the togetherness of I-You. I am one with myself.

4. Decentralization. In everyday life, I experience myself as standing at the center of my world and working to manage and control it. I am preoccupied with my personal agendas and concerns, with my needs and satisfactions, with the way I appear and the impression I make on others. In the transformed state, in contrast, I am part of a larger reality that extends beyond my small self to broader horizons of life. For Marcus Aurelius, I am an integral part of the cosmos, I understand myself as a small entity in the vast cosmos, and I live in accordance with the universal Logos. For Rousseau, I am moved by spontaneous life-energies without self-preoccupation; for Bergson, I am a rivulet in the creative flow of life; and for Buber, I am in togetherness with others and with the world. For all of these philosophers, I live in the name of life instead of in the name of the self-absorbed self.

5. Inner freedom. Before the transformation, I am controlled by fixed psychological forces and patterns, and in this sense I am unfree. After the transformation, as all four thinkers explain, I am free from these mechanisms. Since I am one with myself, there is no gap between me and what my psychological mechanisms tell me to do, between the controller and the controlled within me. Since everything I do and feel and think emerges from a unified source of energies, I am the one who determines myself. For Bergson, my consciousness flows in holistic creative freedom. As a Stoic, I identify with my inner guide and act from it freely. As Rousseau's natural man, my behavior emerges freely and spontaneously out of my natural self. And as a Buberian, I relate to each person in a new and unique way.

To sum up, the four transformational philosophers portray the transformed state as radically different from ordinary moments before transformation. Each moment is precious and full, with a sense of inner unity, openness beyond myself, and inner freedom.

All this, however, might seem merely a matter of subjective state of mind. And a subjective state of mind, as profound as it might be, is not much. Drugs might be able to produce the same effect. However, a closer look would reveal that such a transformation is more than a subjective experience. It also allows us to understand our reality in new ways: The Stoic state of mind reveals to us the ways of reason in the cosmos; Rousseau's natural self allows us to see the human world as it really is, without the distortions of social norms; Bergson's flow of consciousness allows us to appreciate our holistic flow before it was fragmented; and Buber's I-You relations reveal to us the other person in his fullness, as well as the true nature of relations before they have been objectified by distance and separateness.

Thus, the transformed state of mind is not just experiential, it is also a window to a deeper knowledge of our human reality. It allows us to understand the more basic, profound dimension of existence beneath its normally visible surface. The point is not simply that transformation allows us to discover new facets of life, but that it reveals the deeper root of our familiar life. Through self-transformation we come to see the true nature of our existence, the wider context in which our familiar world is located, the basic principles of our life before it became constricted, fragmented, and flattened.

We might say, then, that the inner transformation envisioned by the transformational thinkers gives us a new state of mind which allows us to understand ourselves and our world more profoundly. It opens for us another "dimension" of life, or what can be called the *inner dimension*. And in order to emphasize that this inner dimension is fundamental to human reality as well as largely hidden, it can also be called the *dimension of inner depth*, or *inner depth* for short. Marcus Aurelius' guiding principle, Rousseau natural self, Bergson's holistic flow, and Buber's I-You relations are all different perspectives on—or different theoretical interpretations of—this inner dimension, the dimension of inner depth.

The word "dimension" has to be taken broadly here in order to allow for some diversity. Some philosophers, such as Rousseau and Marcus Aurelius, regard it as an already existing reality that is dormant within us, waiting to be discovered and awakened. Other philosophers such as Nietzsche and Spinoza regard it as an unrealized possibility which awaits realization. For Rousseau, this inner dimension is a fountain of energies, while for Bergson it is a form of organization of our conscious states; for Marcus Aurelius it is a faculty of understanding, while for Buber it is a way of relating to others.

These seem to be different theoretical interpretations of the same basic insight. But regardless of these diverse interpretations, the common insight they share is intimately related to the concepts presented earlier, those of "Plato's cave" and "perimeter." What these thinkers regard as our limited, superficial, artificial, or inauthentic attitudes, each in his own terminology, is what I called our perimeter, or our Platonic cave—our rigid and patterned attitude to our world. The transformation which they encourage us to embark upon is what I termed here transcending our perimeter, or stepping out of our cave.

We may say that the transformational philosophers throughout the ages aim at stepping out of the cave of our normal life, out of our perimeter, and getting in touch with our inner dimension, awakening it, and cultivating it. This goal—especially when formulated in terms of "awakening"—can also be found in various spiritual and religious traditions. What is interesting about the transformational philosophers, however, is their insight that the process of awakening and cultivating our inner dimension can be philosophical, or at least can be aided by philosophical reflection. It can be, in other words, a process of exploring fundamental ideas.

Chapter 8

Glimpses of the Inner Dimension

In the previous chapter we focused on the similarities between different transformational philosophers. It is now time to reflect on the differences between them. As we have seen, these thinkers understand the human perimeter in different terms, propose different ways of overcoming it, and envision differently the inner dimension and the way to cultivate it. These differences suggest that there are a variety of ways to step out of our perimeter, that the process is highly individual, and that it cannot be captured by a single universal formula.

Variety of transformational philosophies

One obvious difference between transformational philosophies is that each of them uses a different network of concepts to understand the human condition. Although they all posit a central dichotomy between our perimetral way of being and our transformed way of being, each one places it in a very different conceptual landscape composed of different concepts.

Consider, for example, the differences between the concepts that populate Rousseau's philosophy and those populating Buber's philosophy. Rousseau understands the distinction between the perimetral condition and the transformed condition in terms of that which originates from within the person versus that which originates from outside him, especially from social influences. The rest of his concepts revolve around this basic dichotomy: On the one side we find ideas such as social mask, interpersonal power games, manipulation, and comparison of self to others through jealousy and pride. On the other side of the dichotomy, we find concepts such as natural desires and natural love, independence, self-motivation, self-sufficiency, genuineness, and spontaneity.

Buber's philosophy, in contrast, places the distinction between the perimetral state and transformed state in a very different conceptual landscape. Since Buber rejects the idea of an isolated "I," his understanding of this distinction has very little to do with Rousseau's distinction between an independent inner self and a social self. The central concepts that make up Buber's world—that of togetherness versus distance, being-with versus thinking-about, total involvement versus partial relations, the other as an object versus the other as a world—have no place in Rousseau's world, certainly not a central place.

Bergson's understanding of the distinction between the perimetral condition and the transformed condition is different from either of these thinkers. Since he is interested primarily in the phenomenology of consciousness, his distinction has little to do with interpersonal relations, and it is, therefore, foreign to Buber's relational concepts. Somewhat like Rousseau, Bergson contrasts inner spontaneity with external influences, but for him these external influences are primarily those of language, not power relations and social comparison as they are for Rousseau. Further, while Bergson's main dichotomy is cast in terms of creative holism versus fragments of fixed units, Rousseau's conceptual landscape is composed primarily of motivational concepts, for example, natural desires versus adaptation to social norms, or self-sufficient versus comparative emotions and motivations. These are obviously very different landscapes of ideas.

Marcus Aurelius is yet different. At first glance, his main dichotomy may seem to resemble Bergson's distinction between two inner states of mind. But unlike Bergson's landscape, Marcus Aurelius' landscape revolves around the distinction between emotional attachment and free rational thought. This distinction has no special status in Bergson's landscape, which is focused on the experiential qualities of mental states, not on their underlying psychological mechanisms. Moreover, in Marcus Aurelius' conceptual landscape, reason and self-control are associated not with the perimetral pole of the central dichotomy as they are for Bergson, but rather with the transformed pole.

To conclude, then, each of the four thinkers we have sampled here understands the perimetral and the transformed states in terms of a different network of concepts. While these conceptual landscapes are not necessarily opposed to each other—they bear, as we saw, some important similarities, at least in spirit—nevertheless they speak in different languages and are composed of different concepts. These are four conceptual landscapes that are made of different building blocks which express different insights, interests, and perspectives. While each one of them is coherent internally—the ideas that compose it fit together nicely—they are not coherent with each other.

Importantly, within each philosophy, the same concepts are used to portray both the perimetral state and the transformed state. For example, in Marcus Aurelius' landscape, the concept of control defines both the perimetral state and the transformed state: While the first is characterized as a state in which emotional desires are in control, the second is characterized as a state in which reason is in control; or, to put it differently, while the rational self is not in control in the first, it is in control in the second. Similarly for Bergson, the concept of fragmentation is crucial in the description of both states: While the perimetral is characterized as a fragmented state, the transformed is characterized as a non-fragmented, or holistic state.

Thus, in each theory both the perimetral and the transformed poles are defined in terms of similar concepts, often as the negation of each other: rational versus non-rational, fragmented versus non-fragmented, togetherness versus separateness. We do not find any serious, coherent philosophy that combines, for example, Rousseau's conception of the perimetral state with Marcus Aurelius' conception of the transformed state. Together the two don't add up to a single coherent conceptual landscape.

Individual differences in Platonic caves

The lesson we can take away from this is that although transformational philosophies all believe in a transformation from a perimetral state to a transformed state, they portray this transformation with networks of concepts that are quite foreign to each other. There seems to be no rational, objective way to decide between those alternative ways of conceptualizing the process. Declaring one of them to be the "correct" way seems to me unreasonably dogmatic. We may conclude that the basic yearning to step out of our cave is universally human, but its translation into specific concepts is not universal. Individuals with different life experiences, different attitudes and sensitivities, and different personal and cultural backgrounds may find different transformational philosophies more or less relevant and applicable.

This suggests that we cannot hope to find one single formula for self-transformation that would apply universally to everybody. Throughout history, both in the East and the West, many religious and philosophical traditions promoted their own vision of self-transformation as the single truth which applies to all. Today, however, we are fortunately much more aware of individual and cultural variations, and we must realize that there cannot possibly be one single road to self-transformation for everybody.

This is why philosophy is a powerful approach in our search for a way out of our perimeter. Philosophy is an open exploration that takes no method or assumption for granted but re-examines accepted formulas, generalizations, and ideologies. It can help individuals explore the basic building blocks of their own unique personal reality. This is also why the philosophical search for self-transformation must be a personal search in which each individual must seek to understand his specific Platonic cave and his specific way of stepping out of it. And this is why philosophical practitioners cannot supply seekers with a set of ready-made ideas, but must approach every individual with an openness of mind, creativity, and sensitivity.

Thus, the philosophical journey is a highly personal journey, both for the philosophical practitioner and for the seeker. It is a search for a personal path that would overcome the seeker's specific perimetral limitations towards a personal relationship with a deeper, hidden, inner dimension of life. There can be, therefore, no question of imposing on the seeker an already-existing view of what this deeper dimension must be. This deeper dimension is something which the individual seeker must explore in a personal way, which can be found only within one's unique reality, and which one must learn to awaken and cultivate.

This dimension is usually hidden and unnoticed, but it does appear in rare moments—rare but still noticeable. It sometimes expresses itself in special moments of silence or exaltation, in vague yearnings, or simply in an underlying dissatisfaction which indicates that somewhere within us we know that there is more to life than we are experiencing now.

Such moments are intimation from another dimension of life which is dormant and waiting to be realized. We live on the surface of our life, but something within us senses that life can be fuller and that it calls us to awaken. Here we should make an important modification to Plato's imagery in his Allegory of the Cave. Although we are usually imprisoned in our cave, we are not totally disconnected from the sunlight outside it, as Plato's allegory seems to suggest. Stray rays of light penetrate sometimes through the opening of the cave, reflect on the walls, and announce that the cave is not all there is to life. And if we notice those sparks of light, then we can awaken to them and start searching for their source.

We have all experienced, I believe, such sparks of "stray light," or intimations from beyond the cave. At the risk of over-simplification or over-generalization, it is worth classifying them to several typical types so that when we search for them we can have a better idea where to look.

Global dissatisfactions

Perhaps the most obvious hint that there is life beyond our narrow perimeter is a general sense of dissatisfaction. A sense of dissatisfaction may be saying to us: "There is more to life than my narrow cave." But not every dissatisfaction is about my cave as a whole. Many everyday dissatisfactions are about specific details *within* the cave, and they express a desire for local changes *within* my usual situation: I want a better salary, I want more time to rest and relax, I'd like my colleagues to appreciate me, I wish I was better looking. In those cases, I am not dissatisfied with the fact that I am imprisoned in a cave—I only wish that my cave was more comfortable, that my shackles were prettier, that my chair was more convenient, that my fellow prisoners were friendlier. These are "normalizing" dissatisfactions, in the sense that they express a desire to improve life within the normal cave.

But sometimes a dissatisfaction is more global, more fundamental. Life may seem to be going well objectively, and yet something does not fully satisfy me. I may have a job that I consider good and secure, I may have a loving family, a nice house and good friends, and yet something is missing.

A general sense of dissatisfaction, not connected with a specific problem, often indicates that something in me is not satisfied with my world—not just with this or that detail in my world, but with my world as a whole. This is a *global* dissatisfaction. It expresses a desire to transform my current horizons of life, to step beyond the boundaries of my perimeter. In this sense, it serves as a call: Something that is beyond my current sphere of life is beckoning me.

Such dissatisfactions are sometimes vague and amorphous, and a person may be unable to explain them except for saying that something is missing in his life. But sometimes they are a little clearer to the person, and their details may hint at the general direction of the hoped-for transformation. For instance, an oppressive sense of loneliness despite having family and friends might hint at a yearning for a Buber-like togetherness with the world; a disturbing sense of dullness and blandness might hint at a longing for plenitude; a distressing sense of inner conflict and indecision might hint at aspirations for wholeness, perhaps like Bergson's. These are mere tentative hints, of course, and we should not impose on them any pre-conceived interpretation. They are starting points for further exploration.

Paula's week follows a familiar pattern. Every morning after a quick breakfast she hurries to work, and at five o'clock in the afternoon she returns home. At home she sits on the couch to rest for a few minutes, and then she gets up and starts preparing dinner. Her husband returns from work a little later and helps her. Her teenage daughter arrives at some point, sometimes with her boyfriend. They eat dinner together, chatting casually about nothing in particular. Then her husband washes the dishes while she watches TV, and when he finishes he joins her until it is time to go to bed.

Day by day the hours fly by quickly with very few novelties in a thoughtless and comfortable routine.

"My life is too comfortable," Paula tells Linda the philosophical practitioner, "without challenges, without passions or even real emotions. I am active and I do things, of course, and I laugh and yell sometimes, but deep inside nothing really matters one way or the other. I almost wish a catastrophe would strike me. It's as if I was..." She searches for words.

"As if you were on automatic pilot?" Linda asks.

Paula hesitates. Then she finds the word and pronounces it triumphantly. "Dreaming—that's the word I was looking for! I feel as if I'm in a dream most of the time."

"A dream? Can you explain to me this metaphor?"

"Well, things are happening like images, not like reality. They are not for real." She falls silent, then adds, "I wish I could wake up."

"What would it be like to be awake?"

"I wish I knew. Perhaps things would be less obvious. Unexpected surprises would hit me over the head. Or shake

me. Or inspire me. I don't know, maybe I'd be struggling for something, really struggling."

"Can you tell me about a recent situation when you felt this sense of dreaming?"

Paula nods sadly. "Like right now, for example. I am talking to you, but I can't make myself feel that it really matters."

Paula's dissatisfaction may offer some initial clues about how her world is constricted, and about the general direction in which it "wants" to be transformed. Her dissatisfaction seems to revolve around the dichotomies of being in a dream versus being awake, comfort versus challenges, a sense of reality versus a sense of as-if, things mattering to me versus things not really mattering. These dichotomies might express both the prison in which she feels imprisoned and the hoped-for transformation.

Of course, these apparent hints must be taken carefully. They may turn out to be false leads. They may be no more than words which Paula has borrowed from a TV program. But they are a good starting point for a serious investigation.

Yearnings

Paula's dissatisfaction suggests that she has a hidden yearning to somehow transform her life. In fact, global dissatisfactions are often accompanied by yearnings: I feel dissatisfied with my life, and I also yearn for a different kind of life. But sometimes the experience of yearning is more pronounced than the experience of dissatisfaction. I may experience a yearning for new horizons more than I experience a negative sense that something is not right. In such cases, it is easier for the philosophical practitioner to investigate the yearning directly.

It is important to distinguish between a yearning and a mere desire. A yearning is about one's life as a whole, about what is perceived to be the foundation of one's life, while a desire is about specific elements within one's life. A yearning is a wish to change the basic coordinates of one's way of living, to elevate life to a higher level, and to make it more than it presently is. It therefore involves a vision—as vague and preliminary and dormant as it might be—about how life could be different.

In contrast, a desire wants to change only a specific element within the person's life, while leaving other elements intact. A desire for a satisfying career, for example, or for economic security, or for a romantic relationship is about a specific element within the scope of the person's life.

Practically speaking, it may be difficult to distinguish between a desire and a yearning. To some extent, this is a matter of degree: The more global and fundamental a desire is, the more it has the character of a yearning. Nevertheless, despite the absence of a clear-cut boundary, there are important differences between the two. A desire is about a specific issue: a commodity to purchase and possess, a relationship to improve, a career to change. A yearning, because of its comprehensiveness, is not about a specific item in life but about the foundation of my life as a whole. We may say that a desire refers to something which I want to *have* while a yearning refers to how I want to *be*. This is the difference between "what" I want to find in my life versus "how" I want to live my life. To use Plato's Allegory of the Cave, it is the difference between wanting to have something within my cave and wanting to step out of my cave towards a new world altogether.

This is why a yearning is usually hard to articulate. Since it is not about a specific item, it cannot easily be described.

Zach is a university student, popular among his friends, socially active, and reasonably successful in his studies. He enjoys hanging around campus, chatting with his many acquaintances and friends, and playing Frisbee or soccer on the campus lawn. He also enjoys going out with friends to the movies, or to a party on weekends.

And yet, underlying his enjoyable lifestyle, he sometimes feels a strange thirst for something more... he cannot find the exact words to describe it. "Something that really matters," he says to himself. *This sense of thirst appears at unexpected moments, sometimes when he is by himself doing his homework, sometimes in the middle of an animated conversation with friends. It stays with him for an hour or two and then fades away.*

One day he notices an announcement about a philosophical self-reflection group that is soon starting on campus, and out of curiosity he decides to join. In the group's first meeting, Linda, the facilitator, suggests to the participants an unusual way of introducing themselves to the group. Instead of giving general personal information— where they live, what they are studying, what their hobbies are—they are invited to describe something they hope to do in their lives.

When it is Zach's turn to speak, he recalls his moments of thirst and decides to share them with the group. "Unlike those of you who spoke before me," he starts, "I can't say I hope for anything in particular. Frankly, I'm quite content with my life, and I don't trouble myself with plans for the future. Still, sometimes I have those moments when I feel that what I am doing doesn't have any real meaning, you know what I mean? And then I wish I could do something more meaningful, something that has... some value, some significance."

"You mean," one of the participants asks, "like helping the poor, or writing a best-seller, or making a scientific discovery?"

"Not exactly. Well, maybe, but it must be something I really ought to be doing. If it's just for the sake of my own amusement or satisfaction, then that's not it. Helping the poor or writing a novel is a great thing to do, but it's not enough. Anybody else could do it instead of me."

"You want to do something different," another participant suggests. "You want to be unique, is that it, Zach?"

"No, I'm not going to count how many people do what I do. I'm not going to give up having children just because everybody else has children. It's more like: I want to feel *that I am doing what I am supposed to be doing, not just an arbitrary project I invented."*

"It sounds to me," Linda notes, "as if you want to be given a mission to accomplish; not just to invent a mission, but to receive it—from God? From the Universe? From Life?"

Zach looks at her in surprise. "Exactly." He blushes. "A mission from life—I like these words."

"It seems, then," Linda adds, "that your experience speaks in the language of an interesting dichotomy: What I invent which is not meaningful versus what I receive from life which is meaningful." Zach nods, waiting for her to continue. "Meaningfulness is the central concept here. It cannot be produced, it can only be given. In such a world, your role is not to invent a mission, but to be faithful to it."

Linda's words touch Zach deeply. They continue to hover in his mind even while the round of introductions continues. After the meeting is concluded, Zach asks Linda how he could further explore this new insight.

Precious experiences

Dissatisfactions and yearnings hint at a possible transformation that is not yet realized. But most of us also experience special moments that give us a taste of what that transformation might be like. For example, in rare moments a magnificent plenitude may engulf us, or we may feel an intense inner silence, or tender love flowing from us towards the entire world, a wondrous fullness, or inspiration, or clarity of mind. These precious experiences tell us that life can be different, and that its potentials are far greater than we normally know. They kindle our yearning for a fuller way of being, and they encourage us to search for a way out of our usual perimeter. But they may also tell us what kind of transformation is possible for us.

Natalie regards herself as fortunate. She has a stable job as an office manager, a loving husband, and two wonderful children, and she has no reason to complain. They are not rich, but their income is sufficient to buy nice clothes and toys for the children, and once a year to take a trip together for several days. Life continues on its expected path, and Natalie feels secure, knowing where it will take her.

One afternoon, at work, a special state of mind invades her. At first she hardly notices it, and she keeps working as usual. But then she notices that an unfamiliar clarity of mind is gradually growing within her. Her awareness becomes clear and intense, her thoughts fall silent, and her bodily actions become precise, focused, effortless as if flowing by themselves. She feels open to the world, to her colleagues, to the customers, even to the walls around her. Everything is now intensely present and vivid, every small object and face and wrinkle, every tiny movement and feeling. She senses that she is seeing the world through new eyes and with a richer understanding than ever, although she cannot articulate this understanding in words.

"This is so rich," she marvels. "I never knew it was possible to see so much."

The experience is soft and fragile, and she holds it within herself carefully so as not to disturb it. She feels that if she ignores it, it will evaporate. For almost an hour she continues working, immersed in this precious clarity. She gives herself to this new state of mind, doing her work steadily and smoothly, without her usual domineering behavior towards her co-workers, without her familiar self-control and self-restraint. She looks at the people around her with a tenderness she had never known, with a sense of understanding and compassion.

After she leaves her office and starts driving home, she notices that her wondrous experience is starting to dissipate. Her mind begins to wonder: What can she make for dinner? When will her children be back at home? She is tempted to dismiss the experience she had just had as a good mood and nothing else, but after further reflection she realizes that it was more than a feeling. No, it elevated her, it opened for her new perspectives, it made her an altogether different person for a couple of hours.

"If I had this state of mind more often," she muses, "I could be a wise woman. I could help people with advice. Maybe I'd even be a guru."

She now knows that she is more than her familiar self. She is not just the usual Natalie. "I can be much more than myself," she whispers. And this "much more" is precious, hidden, maybe dormant, but waiting to be realized. A potential Natalie, a higher Natalie: clear-minded, sensitive, open to all, with a tender calmness and loving wisdom.

She must search for ways to cultivate this higher part of herself, she tells herself. She knows that she cannot force it to reappear, but she would like to open a space for it, to invite it somehow. If only she knew how.

It is only when she reaches home and when the experience is completely gone that its full implication strikes her. She now understands how limited her usual way of being is, how impoverished and bare.

"It's as if I've been blindfolded all my life," she reflects, "and only now I realize it."

Many weeks pass and the memory of her precious experience gradually fades away. What remains in her mind is only the vague sense that her life can be more than it actually is.

Natalie's precious experience is a temporary self-transformation, and it is too brief and isolated to analyze confidently what exactly it tells her about life. Nevertheless, several concepts seem to be central to it: The notion of seeing versus being blindfolded, richness versus bareness, compassionate tenderness versus control, as well as wisdom. Interestingly, in Natalie's experience this wisdom appears to be not for her own sake but as something she could use to help others.

These concepts should be accepted very tentatively and carefully—it is dangerous to put too much weight on one single experience. But we can view this experience as an indication that something within Natalie wants to grow beyond her current boundaries. It is a brief "message" from her dimension of inner depth, a hint that points in a certain direction that needs to be explored and developed. It offers an initial glimpse of a network of concepts which might open her to a new dimension of life.

Earliest memories as a clue to the perimeter and beyond

In addition to global dissatisfactions, yearnings, and precious experiences, it is worth mentioning here a fourth kind of glimpses into the dimension of inner depth: earliest memories. Most of us have two or three early childhood memories from around the age of three to four, more or less. These memories can serve as important clues both about our perimeter as well as about the inner dimension that lies beyond it.

In one respect, an earliest childhood memory is just like any memory from last week or last year—it gives us some information about the person's perimetral understandings. But very early memories have a special significance, or otherwise they would not have been remembered for so many years. After all, in early childhood we experienced dozens of powerful experiences every day, many of them exciting, frightening, painful, funny, or novel. As toddlers, numerous times we fell and bruised our knee, or were scolded or praised by Mom or Dad, we discovered a new kind of animal or toy, we failed or succeeded, missed our parents or were in their arms. And yet, out of these countless experiences, only a handful is still engraved in our memory. It is beside the point whether these memories are true to the facts or whether they express the child's distorted interpretation, or maybe are even pure fantasy. The important point is that they have been present in our memory for most of our lives. This indicates that there is something especially meaningful about them. They were kept in our minds for a reason: because they had resonated with something important within us.

And indeed, in my work as a philosophical practitioner I have been collecting earliest memories—those of counselees, friends, students, and even strangers—and I can say with confidence that in five out of six cases they contain important information about the person's perimeter, as well as about the yearning to go beyond it. Although on the surface they might seem innocent and even uninteresting, a closer look almost invariably reveals a perimetral understanding, as well as a yearning, that play an important role in the person's life. This is usually confirmed by independent explorations.

The importance of earliest memories has been recognized by the psychologist Alfred Adler,[33] a student of Freud who broke away from him and founded a separate school of psychology. However, his analysis of earliest memories is colored by his psychological ideas, which are not relevant to us here.

For our purpose, as I said, an earliest memory has a dual meaning: It offers clues both to the person's perimeter and to the inner dimension that lies beyond the perimeter. In terms of clues to the perimeter, the analysis of earliest memories belongs to previous chapters in which we discussed perimeter analysis. But in terms of clues to the inner dimension, this analysis belongs here, to the present chapter. Since it is hard to analyze one without the other, I postponed the discussion of earliest memories to the present point.

Five guiding principles in analyzing an earliest memory

Analyzing an earliest memory is an art, just like analyzing a person's perimeter in general. Let me suggest here several guiding principles that can help us in this art. First, we can regard an earliest memory as an experience that was *selected* out of many others to be remembered because of its significance. The child's mind "chose" it, so to speak, because it approximated an important understanding or an important yearning.

Norma, a middle-aged woman, is known to her friends for her excessive worries and anxieties. She jealously follows her usual routine and is always nervous about trying new things. She avoids taking trips for fear of

---

33. Alfred Adler, *The Science of Living*, New York: Garden City Publishing Company, 1929, Chapter 5, "Old remembrances," pp. 117-134. John Linton and Richard Vaughan, *Alfred Adler*, London: Faber and Faber, 1945, Chapter 12, "Earliest Recollections of Childhood," pp. 202-218. Heinz Ansbacher and Rowena Ansbacher, *The Individual Psychology of Alfred Adler*, New York: Harper and Row, 1956, pp. 351-357.

accidents; she is afraid of buying new electronic instruments because they might emit dangerous radiation; and she dislikes going out to eat at unknown restaurants because the food might disagree with her or make her sick. Some of her friends suspect that these are excuses she invents to justify to herself why she prefers maintaining her old, familiar habits.

Norma is a distant relative of Linda, the philosophical practitioner. One day, at a family gathering, Linda asks Norma about the earliest memory she could recall.

"*I can think of only one memory from my early childhood,*" *Norma replies.* "*I must have been about three years old because we were visiting my aunt and uncle before they moved abroad. I remember myself looking out of the window to the backyard. There were beautiful flowers all around. I wanted to go out and smell them, so I opened the door and stepped out. At that moment I saw their dog—a Labrador I think, very big, at least for a little child. It was standing there and looking at me, and then it started barking. It was probably a friendly bark, but I was terrified. So I quickly stepped in again, closed the door, and stayed inside.*"

"*Very interesting,*" *Linda says thoughtfully.*

"*Really? I thought there was nothing special about this little anecdote. Every child gets scared sometimes.*"

"*True,*" *replies Linda,* "*but most people don't remember these early episodes. What I find interesting is not the event itself, but the fact that you still remember it. I am sure that at this age, Little Norma had many other experiences, and yet you forgot most of them. It is only this scary experience that you took away with you from that period of your life.*"

"*What are you suggesting?*" *Norma asks.* "*That my memory is the reason I worry so much?*"

"*Well, I don't know which is the chicken and which is the egg. I am suggesting that your mind chose to hold on to this memory because there was something especially significant about it. That memory was not just about a specific dog—it expressed an important idea, probably the idea that the*

world out there is a dangerous place, and that it's better to
stay inside, in your familiar world."

"Yes, I can see that. Better stay inside and miss all those
beautiful things outside. Those flowers—I remember them
to this very day—they were so pretty, almost magical."

"It sounds to me, Norma, that this is another thing your
memory is telling you: that you yearn to go out—not for the
sake of the adventure, not in order to be free, not to prove
yourself, but to find beauty. I wouldn't be surprised if you
secretly yearn for some sort of wonderland."

Norma looks at her surprised. "I certainly do, Linda."

The second guiding principle which is illustrated in
Norma's story is that some details in an early memory are
more important than others. For example, the fact that the
dog looked scary and was barking seems central to the
meaning of this memory. But the fact that the dog was a
Labrador and not a German Shepherd, or that it was
standing on the lawn rather than on sand or gravel, is
probably not very important. This episode was likely
"chosen" to be remembered because of the scary dog, not
because of the lawn. Nevertheless, we should be careful
here. We cannot be sure in advance that the lawn isn't
important for some reason, and that this is why this scene
was selected to be remembered.

Generally speaking, we may assume that most of the
details in an early memory have some degree of
significance, or otherwise they would not have been
remembered throughout the years. For example, if the lawn
was totally unimportant, Norma would probably not
remember what the dog was standing on. The beautiful
lawn might have been part of the beauty of the garden for
little Norma, and part of the appeal to go out and play,
something she was prevented from doing by the dog. We
might therefore say that most of the remembered details
are typically somehow connected to a central perimetral
understanding underlying the memory.

In order to identify this central understanding, it is
helpful to look for details that are out of the ordinary (if

there are such). For example, if the scary dog stood with its back to little Norma, then most likely this would be a meaningful fact. In this case we would ask ourselves: Why was *this* scene remembered, rather than another scene, of a face-to-face encounter with danger?

A third guiding principle to keep in mind is that the emotions associated with the memory are a helpful piece of information. If Norma remembers having been scared of the dog, then the perimetral understanding expressed in this memory is obviously very different from a similar childhood event which she remembers as, say, exciting. Unfortunately, emotions are often forgotten.

Fourth, it is very helpful to look at several early memories, if there are such, and compare them to each other. In my experience, people usually have two or three earliest memories from roughly the same early period. These memories often express a similar understanding (or yearning) in different forms, so that comparing them may help us identify what exactly they express. For example, if Norma also has a second early memory in which she is afraid of getting out of her bed at night because of a scary shadow on the wall, this would confirm the meaning of the dog memory, since they both seem to express the same theme: fear of an outside threat.

However, two memories from the same period do not necessarily say the same thing. They may also be *complementary* to each other. Consider, for example, the memory "I am alone facing a scary dog," and the memory "I am sitting in my mother's lap and looking down at a cute kitten playing on the floor." Why were these two memories selected for memory? What is it about them that is impressive enough to make them noteworthy? A likely answer is that they complement each other, saying: When alone I am in danger, but when with my loved ones I am safe. It may turn out that the first memory expresses a perimetral understanding that the world is alien and threatening, while the second expresses a yearning for warmth and safety. If this is so, then we may need to search for Norma's inner dimension in the direction of loving tenderness.

Lastly, earliest memories contain limited information, and it is impossible to analyze them meaningfully without the help of additional information about the person. A memory in itself is too fragmentary and ambiguous, and only in the context of sufficient acquaintance with the person can we comprehend its meaning. Thus, for example, if we know that the person tends to avoid unknown situations, then this information would suggest that an earliest memory of a confrontation with a dog is saying: "It is best to stay at home, in my familiar, safe place." But alternatively, if we know that the person is adventurous, then the same dog memory may indicate the value of excitement in the face of danger. It follows that an early memory is always a supplement to other sources of information.

Josh's earliest memory is vague, and it is probably from before the age of three. He remembers that he was in bed when his dad entered the room. Little Josh felt an urge to jump out of bed and cuddle in his arms, but immediately he checked himself. Instead, he pretended that he was asleep. He kept still for a while, his eyes closed. That is all Josh can recall from this childhood scene. He doesn't remember exactly what he felt, but he vaguely remembers that it was a pleasant experience.

Looking at this memory, we may ask ourselves: Out of all of Josh's childhood experiences, why was this particular one remembered? What unique theme does it express to make it memorable? Consider first Josh's role in this scene. Evidently, little Josh is not a passive observer; he is not merely looking at something happening. And neither is he a receiver: he is not being given anything, or being carried in his father's arms, or being helped. He is the central actor in the scene, but interestingly his action is not explicit. He is not saying anything out loud, or playing with a toy, or building a castle, or running. Rather, he is hiding himself, pretending.

Often it is helpful to look at what is missing in the memory. In this case, missing is a mutual interaction with

Dad. Although little Josh is not alone—his father's presence is an important element in the story—yet the two are not interacting. Josh is acting upon his father, or even manipulating him.

Also missing in the scene is the reason why Josh pretended to be asleep. Did he do it for fun? Or in order to avoid punishment? Or because he did not want to eat some food his father had brought him? The memory does not answer these questions. It seems that these questions are not important; that the reason for the pretense game was not significant enough to deserve remembering. What impressed Josh was the fact that he could pretend, regardless of why he did so.

These considerations suggest that this scene was remembered because it expressed the idea of pretense and manipulation. It appears, therefore, that this is the understanding that Josh has been carrying within him for so many years: My relation to others (even to my dear ones) is manipulative.

This seems a very appealing interpretation, but as appealing as it may seem, we need to be careful. The memory may have other meanings that are hidden from view because relevant background information may be missing. For example, if the father was a harsh man who was feared by his children, then Josh's pretension to be asleep might have a different meaning, perhaps of escape and survival. Additional information would help to corroborate our interpretation.

As it turns out, Josh has a second memory from about the same age, more or less. This memory is much richer in details: His uncle came to visit them. Little Josh bashfully hid behind his father's legs, but when the uncle smiled at him and patted his head, Josh regained confidence and stepped forward. Then the uncle extended his closed fist and told Josh that he was holding a piece of candy. Excited, little Josh struggled to open his uncle's fist, but when the hand finally opened, it turned out to be empty. Evidently, his uncle had no candy to give him; he was only playing a trick on him. His uncle laughed out loud at his practical joke. Josh burst into tears.

If we examine this second memory, we will see that it supports our interpretation of the first memory, and also complements it. Here, too, Josh's relation to others is manipulative, only this time he is the one who is being manipulated, not the one who manipulates. Clearly, the theme of pretending and manipulating is central to both memories. And if we recall that Josh's memory "chose" these two childhood experiences from thousands of other experiences, we will realize that this theme must be significant in his life. Together, these two memories express the understanding that: "Direct relations are impossible. Either you manipulate or you are being manipulated."

We should not be surprised if we find that Josh, as an adult, displays patterns of pretending, hiding his thoughts, exploiting others, and being distrustful. Needless to say, however, we must also remember that Josh is more than this pattern, and that manipulation may be only one thread in a more complicated perimeter.

Correspondingly, we may also suspect that a related yearning is hiding in these two memories: the yearning for an honest and spontaneous affection, not distorted by manipulation. This is why the first memory portrayed little Josh as suppressing his desire to jump into his father's arms, and the second memory records a moment of trusting. If these hints are correct, then it may turn out that Josh's journey towards self-transformation would benefit from a Rousseau-like network of ideas that revolves around spontaneity and straightforwardness.

Earliest memories in philosophical practice

In philosophical counseling, it is a good idea to ask counselees for their earliest memories, but to start analyzing them only after at least one session, when more personal information is revealed. Analyzing a person's memory prematurely, without any background information, is likely to be distorting. Early memory analysis cannot stand on its own.

When asking counselees for their first experiences, it is important to ask for a specific event that they remember happening, one which they can visualize. For example, "I remember that I used to play alone" is not a specific event but rather a general piece of knowledge about a general habit. It is a good idea to explain to the counselee that earliest memories contain important themes and to analyze them together. In addition to earliest memories, later memories may also be informative, although much less so. Most of us have dozens of memories from the age of seven or ten, and so the significance of any one of them is limited.

Philosophical practitioners can use earliest memories to explore three main things. First, the memory may serve as a clue to the person's patterns. For example, an earliest memory of quarreling may express the person's current pattern of antagonistic behavior. Second, an earliest memory may be used as a clue to the person's perimetral understandings. For example, a counselee's earliest memory about a friend who betrayed her may express her current understanding that people are not to be trusted. These two kinds of clues—clues of a current pattern and of a current understanding—are fairly common, and they typically occur together in the same memory. But a third kind of clue is occasionally found as well. It sometimes happens that an earliest memory expresses the person's longing to go beyond her particular perimeter—beyond her patterns and understandings. Norma's case above is an example.

Chapter 9

Learning the Language of the Inner Dimension

Dissatisfactions, yearnings, precious experiences, and earliest memories—these are the main hints that tell us that our potential life might not be limited to the visible perimeter. There is more to us than our mundane being, namely what I called the hidden depth, or the inner dimension.

But how do we step out of the perimetral prison and get in touch with this inner dimension? What do we need to do in order to awaken and cultivate it?

As a first step, we should learn to identify it, so that we know where to look and what to look for. No general formula can be expected here. Just as the perimeter is different for different individuals, the same should apply to the process of stepping out of the perimeter towards the inner dimension. The inner dimension may speak differently in different individuals. Therefore, in order to learn about my inner dimension, I would need to learn its specific "language" as it speaks in *my* life.

The language of the inner dimension in counseling

Matt goes to see Linda, the philosophical practitioner. After introducing himself, he confesses that he is not sure why he came.

"I guess I am here because I feel confused," he tells her after they sit down.

He has a good-paying job as a technical writer with a high-tech company, but he doesn't feel that this is what he really wants to do. He is good at writing manuals for his company's electronic games, but he often feels that he is wasting his time in this job. The problem is that he can't think what to do instead.

Linda listens and asks a few clarification questions. To his surprise, she also wants to hear about seemingly unrelated things, such as experiences he recently had with his friends, his family, at work.

Towards the end of the meeting, she notes: "It is interesting that a common thread runs through your stories: You are active and you do many things, but you do them half-heartedly. You went out camping with your friends, even though you didn't exactly feel like it. You bought an expensive new camera, but with very little enthusiasm. You accepted a job offer as a technical writer, even though you were not crazy about this kind of work. You even came to see me—so you told me—without knowing exactly why."

Matt ponders, and then shrugs defensively. "I guess I can never figure out what I really want. I wish I could."

In their second meeting, Matt and Linda examine additional aspects of his life, and they realize that this is indeed a prominent pattern in his behavior. At the end of the session, Matt is quite disturbed by this revelation.

"It's terrible, but true," he says sadly. "It's definitely a pattern with me. Very often I feel I'm just guessing what I want to do."

In the following session, Linda takes a new step. So far they have been exploring Matt's behavioral and emotional patterns. Now Linda makes a first step toward the philosophical level, the level of concepts and understandings.

"Let's think about this attitude of 'I don't know what I really want,' as you describe it. What kind of statement does it make about your life?"

"Well, I guess it's saying: Most of the time I'm not in touch with my 'real' me."

Linda nods. "In other words, it is saying that there is a 'real' self in you; that your usual feelings and wants are not as real as what this real self feels and wants."

"Yes, it's like a treasure hiding inside of me."

"A treasure, exactly. And it is very important to be in touch with this treasure—so important, that without it nothing is really worth it. And so, you are passing the time, waiting for this real thing to reveal itself. Life is on hold until then."

Matt smiles pensively. "That's quite a peculiar picture of myself. It's accurate, but peculiar. Still, is there anything wrong with it? Is there anything wrong with wanting only the very best and not settling for less?"

"Not necessarily. My point is that this is your personal way of understanding life, but perhaps not how others understand it. Not everybody is worried about their real self."

"I've noticed that, Linda. When I tell my friends that I don't know whether I really want something, I get the feeling they don't understand what I'm talking about. What do you mean you 'really' want it?—that's how they react. You either want it or don't want it."

"Whereas for you, Matt, there are two different things here: what you think you want and what you really want."

In fact, she goes on to suggest, the concept of realness is central to most of Matt's stories: What I really want, what I really feel, who I really am.

She places a sheet of paper on the table between them and writes on top of it the words "The real me."

This, Matt agrees, seems to be the center of his attitude to himself and to life. "I hope you'll help me understand it a little better."

It is the end of the session, and Linda asks him to think about it at home.

In the next session, Matt admits that he has no idea what or who his real me can possibly be. "I just know I want to be in touch with it. It's hidden. And this hiddenness tortures me. From the outside, everything seems fine with me. At work I talk with the engineers, I learn how the system works, I write the text and send it back for comments. Everybody says I'm doing a great job. But... in the back of my mind I wonder whether all this high-tech business—whether it's really me."

"You make it sound as though there are two Matt's in you: the real Matt and..."

"...and a fake Matt. In my bad moments, that's how I look at myself—a fake."

Linda places on the table the sheet of paper from the previous session and adds to it a second heading at the top, so now it reads: "The real me" and "The fake me."

"Real versus fake," Matt says, "exactly. My colleagues at work all think that I am enthusiastic and that I enjoy the challenges of the job. But it's not coming from my heart. Deep inside I probably don't really care. Do you think I am betraying myself?"

"Betraying yourself—that is an intriguing expression. In betrayal, one person betrays another person. Who is the one who is betraying and who is the one who is being betrayed?"

"Well, the one who is betraying is my usual me, and it is betraying my real me, whatever or whoever it is."

"So again you are telling me, Matt, that in addition to your real self—which is presumably hidden—there is also your usual self, your fake self, which is unfaithful."

She writes a few more concepts on the paper:

"Is this a reasonable summary of the way you understand yourself? It's like a theory you have about yourself."

Matt inspects the chart.

"I've never thought about myself this way, Linda, but yes, you are absolutely right. You summarized the way I relate to myself."

"We can regard it as a theory which you live in practice, without necessarily thinking about it in words. And it obviously raises the question: Who is the 'real' Matt?"

"Yes," he replies after a pause. *"That's exactly the question: Which part of me is the 'real me'?"*

"Do you sometimes actually feel this real Matt? Do you sometimes experience yourself acting without your usual half-hearted hesitation and mistrust of yourself?"

"Sometimes. Not very often. For example, last month I went hiking in the mountains with three of my friends. We wanted to find a small beautiful waterfall we'd heard was there. But we got lost. It was getting late, and we started thinking of turning back home without seeing the waterfall." Matt goes on to describe how he suddenly stood up, took control of the group, convinced his friends to persist, and with surprising resolve and resourcefulness led them to the waterfall. *"For a couple of hours I was full of determination—I don't know where I got it from."*

"It must have felt very good to find the waterfall."

"When we finally found it, I felt this amazing sense of exhilaration. I don't know how to explain it—I was totally one with myself. I was really there, standing on this rock, all of me. Does this make sense to you?"

"It sounds like a precious moment," Linda comments.

Using philosophical texts in philosophical counseling

Matt's experiences tell us about the structure of his perimeter. But some of his experiences might also offer us glimpses of what may lie beyond his perimeter.

At this stage, however, such glimpses are vague. A detailed investigation is needed. An excellent way of doing this is with the help of philosophical texts. Deep philosophical texts are rich with insightful concepts and ideas. They can offer new perspectives and help us clarify our thoughts regardless of whether or not we agree with them.

Linda hands Matt a couple of pages with passages selected from Max Stirner's book The Ego and its Own. *"Here, take this and reflect on it at home. Stirner is not a famous philosopher, but you might find him relevant and provocative. Here he explains his conception of the self and what it means to be authentic, or 'real' as you call it. I wonder, Matt, if this is the kind of realness you are longing for. But first, let me give you a general background about Stirner."*

Max Stirner – the unique self[34]

Max Stirner (1806-1856) was a German philosopher whose writings contain early existentialist, nihilist, and anarchist themes. Stirner argues that the self cannot be defined or described. Any concept that you might want to apply to me is not part of who I really am. I am unique, so that no general concept can capture me. I may be blond, but "blond" is not part of my essence, part of who I really am. I may be happy, but "happy" is not part of who I really am. I may be a man, but "man," or even "human," is not part of who I really am. Therefore, my self cannot be defined, and it is beyond all general descriptions. You may compare my hair color to your hair color, or my human body to your human body, but you cannot compare my self to other selves. I am one of a kind.

This means, argues Stirner, that in order to be true to myself I must throw away anything that is not really me— which is almost everything. In this way I come to "own" myself and only myself. When I do so and become authentically myself, I realize that I do not really fit into any general conception of humankind. Although religions and social ideologies want to impose on me specific identities (you are "human," "a Christian," "a German," "a teacher," etc.), in reality, these are false identities.

---

34. Max Stirner, *The Ego and His Own: The Case of the Individual Against Authority*, Mineola, NY: Dover Books, 2005.

In their next meeting, Linda asks Matt what he thought about the selected paragraphs from Max Stirner.

"I think I see why you chose him for me, Linda. Stirner, too, can't say who he is. But there is a big difference between us: He feels comfortable with this whereas I feel that I am missing something. Are you suggesting I should accept his theory?"

"On the contrary, Matt, I would suggest not to accept or reject anything too hastily. Let us take our time and listen to Stirner's ideas and see whether or not they can shed light on your experiences. Deep philosophical ideas challenge us to think in new ways whether or not we agree with them."

"In fact," Matt says, "the text did make me think. It made me wonder whether the fact that I don't know who I am is really a problem. Maybe it's good not to know. Maybe it means that I am authentic and free from all general descriptions."

"So you are wondering whether Stirner's ideas apply to you."

"Yes, I am."

"Alright. Is the language of Stirner's ideas consistent with the language of your own precious experiences? Think about the concepts he uses, the distinctions he makes, the connections he notes."

"I guess not," Matt ponders. "I don't see myself as a unique person."

"Let's go slowly, Matt, and give Stirner a chance. Recall your waterfall experience and tell me about it as if you were Stirner. Start from the beginning of that day."

"Alright, let's see... In the morning I meet with my friends. We take Bill's car. The three of them chat and laugh and kid around. I'm not in the mood for this sort of socializing, but I play along. Stirner might say that I am quietly preserving my freedom and authenticity and refusing to play social games."

"Is this how you felt in the car?"

"Not really. I wasn't doing anything ideological like that. I simply didn't have the patience to hear their nonsense, but

I was playing along because I didn't want to spoil their mood."

"Alright, go ahead."

Matt continues describing how they park the car, start walking, and get lost.

"Then we notice it's late, and Bill says: 'Let's forget the waterfall and go back home.' And Dennis, too, says something about the sky getting dark. And Mark says he really wanted to see the waterfall, but he's too tired to care. Everybody is starting to feel sort of miserable."

"Good. And what happens next?"

"And then I find myself standing up and saying: 'No, we are not giving up!' Stirner might say that I am asserting my uniqueness, my specialness, my freedom."

"Was there anything in your experience, Matt, that supports this interpretation?"

"Maybe a little bit. I remember a sense of freedom. But it wasn't an issue of my uniqueness, or of rejecting false identities. It was a sense of certainty. That's what I felt when I announced: 'We are not going home. We are going to find the place!'"

"When I listen to your story, Matt, I can't hear your usual hesitation. It sounds as if you found a new personality within yourself."

"That's a good way of putting it. A new personality I didn't know existed in me suddenly erupted to the surface and announced itself. All of a sudden I was a powerful, unified person who knew exactly what he wanted. But this new person was not indescribable, as Stirner would say. I could describe him as adventurous, confident, excited."

"That's a good observation," Linda says. "So perhaps your experience doesn't speak in Stirner's language. Still, is there anything in his philosophy that you are taking away with you?"

"Yes, I'm taking from him the idea that being myself is connected with a sense of freedom, with a sense that I 'own' myself and don't owe anybody anything."

"You are smiling now, Matt. You miss this sense of owning yourself."

"Of course I do. Without it, I feel like nobody."

"Good."

"Excuse me?!"

"Your sense of being nobody is telling you that things are not as they should be. Would it be better if you didn't feel bad about it?"

Linda gives him a reassuring smile and hands him a new text. *"Let's see, Matt, if this text would help you understand yourself a bit more deeply."*

"You think this text has the answer?"

"Of course not. A good philosophical text does not give you answers. It inspires you to understand yourself in your own way."

Jean-Paul Sartre – I am not what I am[35]

Stirner, like many other thinkers, assumes that there is such a thing as a self within each of us. The French existentialist philosopher Jean-Paul Sartre (1905-1980) disagrees. Trying to connect to a "self" inside me is a fantasy or self-deception.

According to Sartre, as a human being I don't have a definite personality, nature, or self. Who I am is something to decide, not something to discover. In other words, there is nothing in me that determines who I am—my values, my beliefs, my inclinations, even my personality—except for my free will. I am free to determine myself. Furthermore, there is no value or morality that can tell me how I *should* be, because values and morality are my own creation. I am completely free to choose who I am, what is good or bad, what I want to do with my life. Even my past does not take away my freedom: If I made a decision ten minutes ago, I am free to change my mind now. Even in jail I can decide what kind of a person I am. In Sartre's words, I am condemned to be free.

In fact, it is inaccurate to say that I am free. More correctly, I am freedom. As Sartre says, I am not what I am

---

35. Jean Paul Sartre, *Existentialism and Humanism*, London: Methuen, 1948.

and I am what I am not. Or, as he also put it, existence precedes essence—in other words, at every point in time I first exist and then I determine my essence (who I am).

All this suggests that authenticity cannot mean being faithful to my inner self. Rather, I am authentic if I am faithful to the fact that *I don't have* a determined inner self; if I am faithful to my freedom to decide who I am. Therefore, being authentic, for Sartre, means that I am aware of my freedom, that I take full responsibility for my life, and don't pretend that some force or fact has made me the person I am. It means that I do not consider myself a product of my psychology, of my education, of the circumstances, of logical or moral consideration, of God. I don't have excuses for being the person I am.

In their following meeting, Matt tells Linda that Sartre's idea of radical freedom is too extreme. "It's obvious to me that I am constrained by my past experiences and by my personality. My psychology dictates many things in my life."

Linda reminds him that the important thing is not whether or not Sartre's theory is correct, but whether it can shed light on Matt's yearning and precious experiences. Even if Sartre's theory as a whole is not acceptable, its main point might still be relevant: that being authentic means being faithful not to something that already exists in him, but rather to his freedom.

For a while they discuss Sartre's theory and its relationship to Matt's experiences. They imagine how the waterfall episode might look from Sartre's perspective: Matt being tempted to give up the search and return home with his friends, but then realizing that he is free to refuse, and through his newly discovered freedom insisting on continuing to search for the waterfall, taking the full burden of responsibility on himself.

"No," Matt finally says, "that's definitely not the language of my experiences. In the waterfall case, it's not as if I suddenly decided to take responsibility. Responsibility is not an issue for me when I feel I don't know what I really want. I am good at taking responsibility. At work, I do all

kinds of creative projects, but this doesn't comfort me. What I long for—I can now see it clearly thanks to the comparison with Sartre—is to be grabbed and guided by a sort of inner conviction. It's not a matter of decision, but of conviction, of a sense of truth, a light to inspire me."

Gabriel Marcel – the witness in me[36]

The French existentialist philosopher and playwright Gabriel Marcel (1889-1973) distinguishes between two attitudes to life: observing and witnessing. An observer is somebody who looks at life without personal commitment, without giving himself to anything. For such a person, life is a sequence of objective, impersonal facts. He may be active and hardworking, but he is not faithful to anything. In a world made only of objective facts, there is nothing to be faithful to.

In contrast to an observer, a witness is somebody who is willing to receive life as if it was entrusted to him. Marcel calls this attitude "testimony" because it is what I do in court when I decide to testify truthfully about something I saw, even if this puts me in danger, even if the court is corrupt. Similarly, I am a witness when I freely accept a certain value or "light" that touches me and am willing to be faithful to it. I take upon myself a commitment to be a witness to this light in my own personal way.

In this sense, life for me is a "gift" which I feel called to receive. But receiving it is not a passive attitude. For example, when I receive guests at home, I am an active, committed, creative receiver, giving from myself to make my guests enjoy themselves. Likewise, when I receive life as a witness, I accept it freely, faithfully, personally, creatively.

In their next meeting, Matt tells Linda that Marcel's notion of "light" fascinates him, but it does not capture what he personally experiences.

---

36. Gabriel Marcel, "Testimony and Existentialism," in *The Philosophy of Existentialism*, New York: Citadel Press, 1995.

"Marcel is too religious for me," Matt explains. "The idea that I should 'receive' a light doesn't mean anything to me: Receive from where? From who?"

"Remember, Matt, that deep philosophical texts help us understand ourselves even by way of disagreement, even when they are very different from what we believe. So let's put aside agreement and disagreement and think about the 'witness' that Marcel envisions—his inner state of mind, his attitude towards life, the way he stands in the world."

"I'm not sure what to say, Linda."

"Then try saying it with your body, with your arms and hands."

Matt stands up and opens his arms towards heaven. Then he puts on his face an expression of supplication.

"Mmm. You are interpreting his 'witness' as being passive, waiting for a miracle from heaven."

"Yes, you're right, Linda. Marcel talks about 'active reception'—like a host who actively receives his guests. He welcomes them, offers them coffee, converses with them."

Matt stands up again and assumes a posture of a host inviting his guests. He sits down.

"Still, this is not what I am longing for. In my waterfall experience and in similar experiences, I felt... I guess 'empowered' is the word. All my uncertainties disappeared, all my familiar hesitations and self-justifications and self-explanations. Ah, yes, I can now see it: In such moments I become one with myself, one unified person. I own myself, as Stirner says."

He stands up again, straight but relaxed. A strange poetic spirit overcomes him. "Everything is calm and simple within me. I am a primordial man in a primordial world, free to love and enjoy, wild, answerable to nothing and nobody."

Linda looks at Matt with a gentle smile. "Wow!"

Matt sits down, somewhat deflated as if waking up from a dream. "Exactly: Wow. For a moment I felt this primordial existence acting in me again, like by the waterfall. Primordial existence—free from complications, free from calculations, just straightforward existence: Everything is real, I am real, I don't have to make up stories about myself."

Linda puts a new sheet of paper on the table between them. "Let's redraw the landscape of your world."

Together, Linda and Matt compose a revised map of ideas:

"This," Linda says at last, "is an excellent starting point for a serious exploration. Now we have the first clues of what you are yearning for, of what it is that calls you, what lies outside your Platonic cave. As far as we can tell at this point, these concepts are the language of your inner dimension."

The inner dimension in philosophical companionships

One-on-one counseling is not always the best format for exploring the language of the inner dimension. The companionship format is sometimes more efficient.

A philosophical companionship[37] is a group of people who meet several times face-to-face or online, usually once a week for one or two hours, focusing on a short philosophical text, preferably condensed or even poetic. A companionship is not a discussion group. What is special about a companionship is that the companions attempt to maintain a contemplative state of mind during the session. With the help of various exercises and procedures, they try to think and converse from their inner depth, not from their automatic thinking patterns or their opinionated mind. Furthermore, instead of expressing opinions, analyzing, and

---

37. For a full discussion how the philosophical companionship functions see Ran Lahav, *Handbook of Philosophical Companionships*, Vermont: Loyev Books, 2016.

judging, they think in togetherness, resonating with each other like jazz musicians playing together. They also resonate with the text, as opposed to talking *about* it.

These three elements—maintaining a contemplative state of mind, resonating in togetherness with others, and resonating with a text—are the core of the philosophical companionship. Thanks to them, the companions go beyond their typical way of thinking, beyond their opinions and automatic thinking patterns, and give voice to aspects of themselves with which they are rarely in touch, especially aspects of their inner dimension.

It is the beginning of the first meeting of a new philosophical companionship facilitated by Linda, the first in a series of sessions on Philosophies of Meaning. The companions are to contemplate in togetherness on short philosophical texts that deal with the meaning of life and in this way gain a deeper understanding of their personal experiences of meaning.

Normally, as the transformational philosophers remind us, we live on the surface of our inner life and are not fully aware of the potential richness and depth of our everyday moments. When we open our minds and hearts and contemplate in togetherness on a selected philosophical text, the text opens us to new horizons of meaning. One might say that the goal of the companionship is to awaken an additional dimension of life—additional depths—that are normally hidden from view.

This evening, the companionship focuses on a short excerpt from Albert Camus.

Albert Camus – To experience more[38]

In his book *The Myth of Sisyphus*, the French Existentialist philosopher Albert Camus (1913-1960) asks whether life is worth living. Camus responds that the world as we experience it is "absurd"—devoid of meaning and

---

38. Albert Camus, *The Myth of Sisyphus and Other Essays*, New York: Vintage Book, 1991.

values. Doctrines about God, about the afterlife, morality, and meaning are mere speculations or human inventions. The only thing we know for sure, the only thing we can rely on, is what we experience directly.

This implies that any value-judgment about my behavior would have no basis in reality. What matters is not whether my action is noble or vulgar, good or bad, but rather whether it allows me to have direct experiences of life. What counts is whether the action gives me the only thing I know to exist: experiences. As Camus puts it, the important thing is not "better experiences" but "more experiences": a richer variety of situations which I experience fully, consciously, passionately.

In short, according to Camus a situation is meaningful to the extent that it gives me new powerful experiences, if it allows me to experience life more fully and passionately.

Linda hands out copies of a one-page excerpt from Camus' book, and the group reads it together. Each participant reads one sentence, slowly and out loud, according to their sitting order. When they finish reading the text, a few seconds of silent re-reading allow them to contemplate the text as a whole.

"Needless to say," Linda explains, "we don't have to agree with Camus. In fact, tonight we will not agree or disagree at all. Let's put aside our personal opinions and simply listen to what the text tells us and to the understandings that the text arouses in us."

She places a sheet of paper at the center of the circle and writes on it the word "Meaning."

"This is obviously the central concept in this text," Linda explains. "Which additional concepts do we find here? I am asking because we want to understand Camus' landscape of ideas and to note the main landmarks in this landscape. But in order to answer this question, let us not analyze the text in the abstract. Let us not limit ourselves to opinions and logical thinking. Let us contemplate, which means thinking from our inner depth, giving voice to deeper understandings within us."

Linda now gives a short meditative centering exercise in order for the group to enter a contemplative mode. In this exercise the participants use their body as a metaphor for their entire being. They close their eyes, focus on the flow of air coming in and out of their nostrils, and slowly descend along the column of air into their mouth, to their throat, their chest, their stomach, and finally to an imaginary point underneath their bodies.

This meditative exercise is short, and after five or ten minutes the participants slowly open their eyes and relax.

Linda starts speaking again, but in a quiet, peaceful way. "Let us start contemplating on the landscape of Camus' text, and do it in togetherness. This means that I don't argue with you, I don't possess an opinion, I don't have an idea of my own. Everything I say is one strand in the thinking of the group as a whole, one voice in our choir. We want to resonate with each other like jazz musicians playing together."

For this purpose, Linda introduces a procedure called "Precious Speaking": You must speak sparingly as if each one of your words is precious, each word is a gift to the group. You avoid repetitions, excessive explanations, and redundant words. One sentence is usually enough to say what you need to say. And when others speak, you open a space of silence inside you and listen from it.

Using this procedure, Linda now invites the companions to present a concept that strikes them as important in the text.

"The concept of experience," *Larry offers slowly.*

Linda writes down the word "experience." *Then she turns to him again.* "And now, please explain it in one sentence."

"When I have a meaningful moment, I have a deep experience."

"The concept of newness," *Hilary says.* "My moments are valuable to me if they are new and fresh and noticeable."

After a long silence, Dan speaks. "Absurd," *he says.* "Even though life is absurd, an absurd life is still worth living."

After several additional statements, when everybody has spoken at least once, Linda makes a sign to stop.

"Good, we now have an inventory of concepts," she says. "Let us try to consolidate it."

She invites the participants to select from the inventory those concepts that strike them as most important. To do so, they do not explain or justify themselves, only repeat the concept they had selected. A handful of concepts emerge, and Linda writes them in large letter on the sheet of paper, omitting the rest.

"This network of ideas is like a map. It is our map of the landscape of Camus' world. Now that we are beginning to see this landscape, let us take a step into it. Let's walk in it and look at it from the inside."

Mentally, the participants push aside their usual opinions and their usual attitudes and ideas, and imagine themselves entering Camus' mind.

"Now that we are inside," Linda says, "and are walking together in that landscape, you are invited to share with us—still in Precious Speaking—what you see around you: interesting landmarks, distinctions and oppositions, hidden implications, connections."

Like a group of travelers walking together in a new world, the companions share observations about the nature of meaning as it appears in Camus' world. They note several kinds of situations that are especially meaningful in that world, they wonder about the place of love and friendship, and they reflect on the connection between meaning and freedom. For some ten minutes they speak in Precious Speaking spontaneously, without turns.

"Good," Linda summarizes this exercise. "And now that we have in mind the outlines of Camus' conceptual landscape, let us try to relate it to our own personal lives. Try to recall an everyday experience you recently had which was quite meaningless to you—nothing dramatic, perhaps a pointless argument, perhaps a waste of time while waiting for somebody who didn't show up. Please bring this situation to your mind."

For a few moments the companions reflect in silence on their selected experiences. Then volunteers are invited to describe their experience to the group. In order to remain in a contemplative state of mind, they limit themselves to only two or three condensed sentences.

David is the first to speak. "A couple of friends came over last night, and we chatted and had some beer. It was cozy and comfy, but nothing really happened, nothing we said was worth remembering, no sense of intimacy."

"Thank you, David," Linda says. "And now, let us all imagine ourselves in David's living room last night. You may close your eyes if you want to intensify your imagination. You are now with David, sitting with his friends, chatting lazily, a beer in your hand. You feel the cozy laziness in your body. And you also feel the sense of meaninglessness in your mind and heart."

For a few moments the participants silently let their imagination take them to David's room. Then Linda invites them to change David's story: to enrich it with elements of meaning from Camus' philosophy.

"I am in David's living room," Heidi speaks thoughtfully. "But suddenly I am no longer lost in chattering about nothing. I am fully aware of the chatter, I experience intensely every word and every sound. It's marvelously rich."

"I am aware of my feelings and images," Jeff adds. "My mind is no longer empty."

"I follow every tiny thought in my awareness," Heidi speaks again. "I know that in the grand scheme of things what is happening to me now is absurd. And yet, I savor every bit of experience."

The companions savor the imagined experiences and feel them powerfully in their contemplating mind while remembering the context of Camus' text. They feel as if they are hovering in a different world. A few minutes later, at the end of the brief exercise, David thanks everybody for visiting his world, and they all move on to the next companion, Heidi, to enter the meaningless moment she had chosen.

When the round ends, after four or five volunteers had the opportunity to share their personal experience, the companions relax and share with the group what they are taking away with them from this exercise. Not surprisingly, none of them has become a follower of Camus. They have traveled together into Camus' landscape and have enriched their understanding of meaningful experiences from Camus' perspective.

The last twenty minutes of the session are devoted to a concluding conversation about the meeting and about Camus's ideas, and it is no longer constrained by contemplative guidelines. Most of participants agree that this deep contemplative experience has enabled them to learn vividly, in the intimacy of togetherness, some potential ways in which meaning can express itself in their daily lives.

In their second meeting, Linda introduces a different procedure, but with a similar aim: to contemplate potential forms of meaningfulness. This time, she wants the companionship to start with a more detailed and organized understanding of the text. Before starting to read it together, she makes several introductory remarks on it.

Erich Fromm – overcoming our isolation[39]

In his book *The Art of Loving*, Erich Fromm (1900-1980), an influential thinker and humanistic psychologist, explains that our central need is to overcome our isolation. Our capacity to reflect on ourselves makes us aware that we are separate entities, separate from nature, separate from other human beings, and separable from our loved ones because of the prospects of death and other uncontrollable circumstances.

This creates in us a tremendous anxiety, which Fromm describes as the root of all anxieties. Consequently, we keep trying, in a variety of ways, to overcome our separateness by connecting to others and to the world. Some of these

---

39. Erich Fromm, *The Art of Loving*, New York: Harper & Row, 1989.

ways are destructive: conformity with the group, for example, or fusion with a nationalistic ideology, or distorted relationships of dependence and loss of self. They are destructive because through them we lose our personal freedom and identity.

But other ways of overcoming our separateness are deeply meaningful: creativity connects us to worlds beyond our immediate reality; true friendship and true love connect us to other people. These are meaningful experiences to the extent that they allow us to transcend our boundaries, while at the same time to preserve—and even enhance—our integrity and personal identity. In real love we actively express our ability to give from the center of our being, thus expressing our personal potency and individuality.

It can be said, therefore, that meaningful situations are those in which we overcome our separateness without losing our identity. Fromm says that one of the most meaningful and exhilarating experiences in life is when the wall between me and another person breaks down and we feel togetherness and union.

The text which Linda has selected from Fromm contains five paragraphs. The group contemplates each paragraph separately, and after each paragraph the companions are invited to articulate, in the procedure of Precious Speaking, the central idea which they can discern in that paragraph. At first, the companions voice a variety of different statements, but after a while the statements start converging on a common theme, although not to a complete consensus. As Linda puts it, the result is not a single idea, but a symphony of interrelated ideas.

The contemplative process of Precious Speaking enables the companions to open themselves to some of the ideas in the text, to reflect on them deeply within themselves, and to resonate with them and with each other. After about thirty minutes, when they finish contemplating on the main idea in each paragraph, Linda poses a concluding question, to be answered in the Precious Speaking procedure: Considering everything we have read and said so far, what you are taking away from Fromm's text?

"Fromm is telling me," David says, *"that meaning speaks in the language of isolation versus togetherness, separateness versus being-with."*

"And in the language of anxiety too," Hilary adds. *"Anxiety gives me a sense of urgency to break the walls that surround me and to connect with others."*

Other participants speak too, and the round of Precious Speaking continues for a few more minutes.

Now that the group has a richer understanding of the text, Linda wants the participants to relate it to their own personal experiences. She asks them to try to remember a recent personal experience which resonates with something in Fromm's text. She asks them to quietly read the text with this task in mind.

After a few moments, when everybody seems to have found a personal experience, she interrupts the silence saying, "What does the personal experience you have found tell you about your sense of meaning? Did it speak in exactly the same language as Fromm's concepts? If not, then in what language did it speak?"

She pauses, then adds, "But instead of answering this question with many words, let us do it in poetry. Poetic words require us to listen inwardly, and they can sometimes express what a straightforward explanation cannot. So let us write a group poem, all of us together. Each one of us will compose two verses, and then we will put all our verses together into one unified philosophical poem. A poem is always more than its individual verses. The whole contains new meanings that emerge from the interaction between the lines."

For several minutes the participants concentrate silently, each one trying to envision the experience they had selected and give it a poetic expression. They write down their poetic verses in their notebooks, and later copy them to a common sheet of paper one under the other.

The resulting group-poem is surprisingly rich, but also somewhat inconsistent. The different contributions do not always fit together. The group therefore works to change the order of the verses and adjust them to each other by unifying pronouns and tenses. The result is an inspiring poem. The companions read the poem together, and in an open conversation reflect on its implications. They all feel that this exercise has shed a new light on their personal sense of meaningfulness.

"So far," Linda says at the beginning of the companionship's third session, "we have been contemplating ideas developed by historical philosophers. Today, let us focus more fully on our own personal sense of meaning. But first, let us enrich our repertoire of historical ideas. We have talked about Camus' idea that meaning comes from the richness of experience, and about Fromm's idea that meaning comes from the love that takes us beyond ourselves. What about meaning as coming from success, struggle, achievement?"

William James – the struggle for an ideal[40]

In his lecture "What makes life significant," the American psychologist and philosopher William James (1842-1910) argues against two conceptions of meaning. On the one hand, he rejects the view that we get a sense of meaning when our needs are satisfied. After all, when we have everything we need physically and emotionally, with no struggle or difficulty, then life is boring and empty. On the other hand, James also rejects the view, which he attributes to Tolstoy, that every struggle and hardship is necessarily meaningful. James reasons that a hardship that is not directed at a goal or ideal is pointless and dull. It is significant only if it has a purpose.

A meaningful situation is therefore characterized by two elements: First, it contains struggle, persistence, determination. Second, it also contains an ideal towards which the struggle is directed. James is talking here not just

---

40. William James, "What makes life significant," in: J. McDermott (ed.), *The Writings of William James*, Chicago: University of Chicago Press, 1977.

about dramatic struggles for glorious ideals, but also about mundane struggles for better living conditions, for success at work, etc.

The inner attitude involved in such a struggle is explained in another text by James in which he discusses the will.[41] James explains that normally, all kinds of ideas in our mind influence our behavior. However, in a meaningful struggle we keep a specific idea vivid in our mind with the effort of attention. We hold on to this idea and in this way overcome our tendency to slide to easier, safer, more comfortable paths.

A meaningful action, therefore, involves a mental effort—an effort to fix our attention on an ideal and disregard other distracting ideas, such as those expressing doubt, fear, or laziness.

For a while the companions sketch together the network of concepts that are central to William James' approach, using the Precious Speaking procedure. They identify as central to his approach the concepts of struggle, ideal value, persistence, and attention.

Now Linda places on the table the three conceptual maps of the three thinkers they had considered so far, Camus, Fromm, and James. "This is our inventory of ready-made concepts. We will use it as a starting point to reflect on our own personal conception of meaning."

She asks each one to think about three experiences they have had recently that were preciously meaningful, and also about two-three that felt meaningless, boring, empty.

After the participants silently construct a short list of personal experiences, she adds, "And now I would like each of you to reflect on your selected experiences and bring them together into one unified 'theory' of meaning. To do this, try to identify what is common to all your meaningful experiences and distinguishes them from all your non-meaningful experiences. This will be a preliminary draft of

---

41. William James, 'Will," in: J. McDermott (ed.), *The Writings of William James*, Chicago: University of Chicago Press, 1977, pp. 684-716.

your personal theory about what is meaningful and what is not meaningful."

This time, the participants work in small groups of three or four participants. In order to maintain a contemplative attitude, they limit their interaction to condensed speaking and to focused listening to each other. When they finish, they return to the main circle and share their lists with each other.

Linda now concludes the day's activity.

"Today we made another step towards understanding the 'language' of our experiences of meaning. In the togetherness of our group, and with the help of historical texts, we learned about different conceptions of meaning and about our own conception of meaning."

"And what are we going to do with what we have learned?" Angela asks. "The experiences we examined are very special. They may be precious, but they don't happen to us very often."

Linda nods in agreement. "You can regard these experiences as little gems in the midst of our everyday life. If we don't want to be stuck in routine everydayness, if we don't want to live on automatic pilot, on the surface of our being, in our Platonic cave, then we need to be aware of those special moments. They offer us glimpses of something very important. They help us remember that it is possible to live more fully. They invite us to develop the deep aspects of our being which we usually neglect. This is what I call 'the inner dimension' or our 'inner depth.'"

Paul appears to be pondering. "So how exactly do we find this inner dimension, or inner depth, Linda?"

"I don't think, Paul, that it is the sort of thing that can be captured with a universal formula. Each one of us must explore it himself or herself. I hope that in our three sessions so far, we started to understand the language of our personal inner dimension—the language of our longing, of our precious experiences, of our sense that life can be more than it actually is. I hope that we are beginning to understand what our inner depth is saying."

The companions agree. To be sure, understanding the language of the inner dimension is not yet awakening it, but it is an important first step.

"And let us also remember," Linda concludes, *"that our inner dimension is not a fixed structure. It is not something we can grasp once and for all. It may change and grow and develop through our lifetime, it may unfold and reveal itself little by little through life-events. It may also be influenced by what happens to us and by what we do: by our decisions, by the attitudes we assume, by the lifestyle we adopt, by our open-mindedness or closed-mindedness, by our love, and by the wisdom we acquire through life."*

"My inner dimension is a living thing," Heidi suggests.

"Indeed," Linda replies, *"But it is not exactly a 'thing.' It is not something I have. It is me, my innermost me."*

Chapter 10

Cultivating the Inner Dimension

By now we are able to understand the structure of a person's perimeter, as well as the language of the inner dimension which lies beyond it. But this still seems a theoretical kind of understanding. The question is how to put this theoretical understanding into practice and translate it into real self-change.

The gap between theoretical self-understanding and self-change might seem enormous, but in fact it is not unbridgeable. Throughout history we find that contemplation of theoretical ideas has been used for self-transformation in many wisdom and spiritual traditions, both in the East and in the West. The ancient Gnostics,[42] for instance, who flourished at the beginning of the first millennium, believed that secret knowledge can liberate the sparks of divine light that are hidden in our being and elevate us to higher levels of reality towards the divine. In fact, this is why they were called "Gnostics"—a word that comes from the same root as the English "know" and that means "knowers." Likewise, in Judaism, reflection on the holy Talmud is an important daily activity for Jewish men (and recently for women as well) as part of the person's formation. The daily reflection serves to mold the person's attitude to life by creating in his mind a rich network of ideas that involve all aspects of everyday life, from toilet

---

42. James Robinson (ed.), *The Nag Hammadi Library*, New York: HarperCollins, 1990. For a moving prayer of thanksgiving after receiving revealed knowledge see "The Prayer of Thanksgiving," pp. 328-329.

activity to prayer, from insects to machinery.[43] An example from the Christian world is the Lectio Divina,[44] a four-stage contemplative reading of the scriptures, first developed in the Middle Ages by Carthusian monks. This practice is designed to produce profound spiritual insights and a sense of intimacy with God as part of one's spiritual growth.

These three Western examples—the Gnostic experiential knowledge, Talmudic analysis, and Christian text-contemplation—are different ways in which reflecting on ideas can be transformative. None of them, however, is strictly speaking a *philosophical* activity. An activity can count as philosophizing only if, at the very least, it involves an open-minded exploration of fundamental life-issues without a commitment to already-existing doctrines and with a willingness to question all assumptions and authorities. In contrast, religious contemplation takes for granted certain religious doctrines, scriptures, and authorities without questioning their validity. Nevertheless, these traditional practices serve as a testimony to the transformative power of contemplation.

Transformative contemplation in Marcus Aurelius' *Meditations*[45]

In the philosophical tradition of the West, several approaches use the transformative power of philosophical reflection. An especially fascinating example is found in the *Meditations*, written by the Roman philosopher and emperor Marcus Aurelius. The *Meditations* is a Stoic book that contains some central ideas found already in earlier

---

43. Joseph Soloveitchik, *Halakhic Man*, Philadelphia: Jewish Publication Society of America, 1983.
44. For modern forms of this practice see Gustave Reininger (ed.), *Centering Prayer in Daily Life and Ministry*, New York: Continuum, 1998.
45. Earlier versions of this chapter were published in Spanish as "Auto-Conversación de Marco Aurelio en las Meditaciones: una lección para la práctica filosofía," *Sophia: Revista de Filosofía* (Ecuador) 5, 2009, and in English as "Self-Talk in Marcus Aurelius' *Meditations*: a lesson for philosophical practice," in *Philosophical Practice* 4, 2009, pp. 486-491.

Stoic writings, and it reformulates and develops them in an engaging way.

Pierre Hadot[46] and A.A. Long,[47] two prominent historians of ideas, interpret the text as a personal notebook of Stoic exercises, or what Hadot calls "spiritual exercises."[48] According to them, Marcus Aurelius' primary purpose in writing this notebook was not to speculate but rather to practice, not to *record* his thoughts and attitudes but to *influence* them. In this sense, the *Meditations* can be seen as one of the ancient precursors to modern philosophical practice.

Consider, for example, Marcus Aurelius' words in Book 2, section 9 of his *Meditations*:[49] "This you must always bear in mind: What is the nature of the whole, and what is my nature, and how this is related to that, and what kind of a part it is of what kind of a whole; and that there is no one who can hinder you from always doing and saying the things which are according to the nature of which you are a part."

The first few words in this passage—"This you must always bear in mind...."—like many similar ones throughout the book, indicate that the writer is addressing somebody. That somebody is himself. Marcus Aurelius is telling himself to prepare for the hassles of the day by contemplating on the universe and on his own small part in it. By writing down these words, he attempts to influence his thoughts, attitudes, and behaviors so that they would follow the Stoic ideals. This is part of his Stoic program of self-transformation towards inner peace and harmony with the cosmic Logos.[50]

---

46. Pierre Hadot, *The Inner Citadel: The Meditations of Marcus Aurelius*, Cambridge: Harvard University Press, 1995. See especially pp. 28-53.

47. 1998. A. A. Long, *From Epicurus to Epictetus. Studies in Hellenistic and Roman Philosophy*, Oxford: Clarendon Press, 2006.

48. *The Inner Citadel*, Chapter 3, pp. 35-53.

49. Adapted from *Meditations*, Amherst: Prometheus Books, 1991, Book 2. I replaced older pronouns and inflections with modern ones for the sake of ease of reading.

50. Pierre Hadot, *The Inner Citadel: The Meditations of Marcus Aurelius*, Cambridge: Harvard University Press, 1995, pp. 35-53.

The exercises employed in the *Meditations* are of several different kinds. Some of them aim at developing self-control, others at developing rational judgment, self-awareness, moral behavior, fulfillment of duties, etc. Overall, however, their point is similar: to bring to awareness certain Stoic ideas and in this way give them the efficacy to guide the writer throughout the day.

This, however, raises an intriguing issue: What is the point of saying to yourself an idea which you already know? If you already understand how you should think and behave, then what is the point of writing this down to convince yourself?

The answer is that Marcus Aurelius regards the soul as divided into two parts: the rational and the irrational parts of himself. The first already believes in Stoic principles, and it speaks to the second part, which is not yet convinced. This latter, irrational part consists of stubborn psychological mechanisms which tend to control our body and states of mind and are governed by various psychological and biological forces, parallel to what I called our "perimeter." These include, for example, our pain and pleasure patterns, our emotional reactions, and the desires which they automatically produce. Since they are governed by irrational forces and not by our free will, they are not considered by Marcus Aurelius to be fully ours.

In contrast, the rational element in the soul is free from psychological forces and mechanisms. This is the "guiding principle," or "daemon." In line with Stoic philosophy, it expresses our true human nature—reason, which is in harmony with the Logos that runs the entire cosmos. As the rational principle within us, it can examine our situation rationally, evaluate it and decide how to act and react. For Marcus Aurelius, only the rational self is free. It is therefore the only element that is truly me, my real self.

However, even this distinction, between the guiding principle and psychological mechanisms, cannot fully explain why Marcus Aurelius is speaking to himself. If his psychological mechanisms are not in his control and do not operate in accordance with rational reasons, then it makes no sense to speak and write to them. Non-rational mechanisms cannot be spoken to and cannot be convinced by philosophical considerations. Indeed, in his exhortations he tells himself to dissociate himself from psychological mechanisms.[51]

This suggests that the speaker in the *Meditations*—which is presumably Marcus Aurelius' rational guiding principle—is talking to itself, not to the irrational part. But if so, then we are back to our initial question: What is the point of telling our self an idea which it already understands? What is the point in trying to convince a self that is already convinced?

This question, however, is formulated in a misleading way. It assumes that Marcus Aurelius' self-talk is designed to convey ideas to somebody. As long as we accept this assumption, it is hard to see who that somebody might be. The way out of this problem is to realize that the goal of his self-talk is not to talk *to* himself, but rather to talk *from* himself. His self-talk is effective not because his true self hears his ideas, but because it speaks them. By encouraging the guiding principle to express itself, Marcus Aurelius gives voice to it, awakens it, and strengthen it.

Opening an inner clearing through contemplation

Marcus Aurelius' exercises teach us an important lesson: that we can empower the deeper aspect of ourselves—our inner depth, our inner dimension—by giving voice to it and encouraging it to express itself. They teach us that philosophical ideas have the power to change us, provided they are not confined to abstract thinking, but are made to involve our deeper self.

In order to utilize this idea in philosophical practice, we must first distinguish between the methodology of Marcus Aurelius' exercises and his Stoic approach to life. He applies his contemplative methods to Stoic ideas, but we, who are not committed to Stoicism, can use his methods without

---

51. See for example *Meditations*, Book V, section 26, and Book XII, section 3.

accepting this particular philosophy. In philosophical practice we do not want to impose any pre-given doctrine on the philosophical journey. Our aim is to awaken the inner dimension but to give it the freedom to search for its own unique way. Therefore, instead of using Marcus Aurelius' exercises in the name of one single doctrine, we should use them with a variety of alternative ideas and allow our inner depth to grapple with them, experiment with them, and choose or create its own path.

On the other hand, our inner depth is not likely to be inspired by any arbitrary idea. It can be touched only by ideas that are sufficiently close to it and with which it can resonate. Therefore, if we want to awaken our inner depth in a non-dogmatic way, if we want to inspire it to explore its personal path out of the Platonic cave, then we must touch it with philosophical ideas that speak in languages similar to its own. For example, if my inner dimension is oriented to the concepts of empathy and solidarity but not at all to the idea of aesthetic beauty, then it is not likely to be moved by reflecting on philosophies of aesthetics. Therefore, if we know the language of the person's inner dimension, if we know the main concepts that underlie its vision and orientation, then we can use philosophical texts that contain similar ideas in order to awaken and inspire it.

This does not mean that we must know in advance which philosophical theory would be the right one for a given person. There is no harm in trying various alternatives, especially since it is impossible to know exactly how a person's inner dimension is capable of developing. Like a baby who is only starting to explore itself, the inner dimension does not know in advance its own preferences. As long as we keep an open mind, are sensitive to the person's reactions, and are ready to change our course whenever appropriate, we have a good chance of finding a path into his inner dimension, his inner depth. Especially fruitful are texts or ideas that are related to basic life-issues—in other words that are philosophical, since reflecting on them is likely to resonate with the person's most fundamental yearnings and struggles.

Reflecting on ideas from our inner dimension is *contemplating*. Unlike ordinary forms of thinking, contemplating means that we silence our normal thinking patterns, open an inner space, and allow our inner dimension to do the thinking. Philosophical contemplation on relevant ideas is, then, a powerful way to give voice to our inner dimension, arouse it, and in this way inspire it to reach out to beyond our perimeter.

I call this general approach to stepping out of one's Platonic cave *The Way of Philosophical Contemplation*. It consists of, first, exploring the language "spoken" by one's perimeter and inner dimension; and second, using related philosophical texts to awaken the inner dimension by giving it voice, or more specifically by contemplating philosophically on the fundamental concepts that preoccupy it.

Contemplation is not an easy practice. It is not something we can do simply by going through certain motions. As Marcus Aurelius shows us, in order to contemplate effectively we must develop our ability to open ourselves to the power of ideas. We should learn, in other words, to respond to ideas not with our perimetral patterns of thought but using our inner dimension, our inner depth. To use a geographical metaphor, we must listen and respond to ideas "from" a different "place" within us, namely an aspect of ourselves which is not controlled by our automatic perimetral patterns. The more fully we develop this capacity, the more we are able to put aside our perimetral reactions and allow new understandings to act within us and transform us.

It would be unrealistic to expect my perimeter to completely melt away. I am, after all, a human being—a creature with a specific psychological structure and biological constitution, influenced by my specific culture, language, and personal history. Even after much practice, many of my emotions and behaviors will continue to be governed by my perimetral understandings and will, therefore, limit me to certain emotional and behavioral patterns. And yet, these perimetral patterns will not completely dominate me as long as I manage to ensure that at least certain aspects of my being, at least sometimes, are not governed by them.

My task, therefore, is to learn to open within myself a space that is empty of my perimetral self, free from my normal rigid and narrow attitudes. We might call this a *clearing* in the forest: an open space in the midst of the dense network of my perimetral understandings. As the metaphor of "clearing" suggests, the point is not to abolish my perimetral "forest" but to create a free patch within the forest, as small as it might be, that opens to the sky. This would allow me to assume a different inner attitude to life at least sometimes, at least in certain situations. And this local, temporary clearing could enable philosophical understandings to animate me, inspire me, and nourish me. A few rays of light that penetrate through the foliage can sometimes illuminate the entire forest.

In some cases, a clearing is like a "gift" which we "receive" unexpectedly, as if by itself, like a passing mood, independently of our efforts. It sometimes happens, for example, for no apparent reason, that we feel endowed with immense sensitivity and clarity of mind. Ordinary events appear to us full of new meanings, surprising insights rise within us and inspire us, and we are touched in new ways by sights, by words, by people and landscapes. This may be accompanied by a sense of inner silence, of focus, harmony, or an effortless flow. It is as if our usual state of mind has been pushed aside, and a new wondrous plenitude is taking its place for a few minutes or hours.

A clearing, therefore, does not always depend on us. Nevertheless, to a considerable extent we can facilitate its appearance with our own efforts. The least we can do is to pay attention. Clearings appear in our minds more often than we realize, but we are usually too busy to notice them. Our usual patterns and conceptions are too powerful, and they quickly take over before we note that something significant has just happened. Even when we notice a clearing, we often dismiss it as nothing but a pleasant mood. But when we notice it and cultivate it, then we experience a small miracle. It is as if our world assumes new horizons that extend far beyond our usual self.

In addition, clearings can be the fruit of practice. Through ongoing experience we can gradually learn to push back our normal perimetral forces and open a free space within ourselves, at least for a while. Through daily practice we can then learn to be involved in the world, in our everyday work and errands, and at the same time be bigger than our small perimetral self.

Opening a clearing is not yet contemplating, certainly not philosophically, since by itself it does not involve philosophical ideas. But when we maintain a clearing within us, even for a short duration, our philosophical reflections can become truly contemplative.

Contemplating with a philosophical text

For more than twenty years I have been exploring contemplative techniques, partly by myself, partly in various monasteries, and partly in philosophical workshops and retreats in many countries. My experience has taught me that philosophical texts can be a powerful aid in contemplation. A good philosophical text presents us with a rich network of ideas about fundamental life-issues. As such, it can help us look at the foundation of our perimetral life from new perspectives and depths.

There are many text-based exercises that can be used to awaken our inner dimension and give voice to it. Through these exercises we can examine concepts, articulate questions, compose ideas, notice assumptions and connections—and do so not from our ordinary opinionated self, not from our automatic thinking patterns, but from our inner dimension. Such an activity is truly contemplative because it allows us to push aside our usual way of thinking and let deeper insights arise within us.

When we use a philosophical text for text contemplation, we do not regard it as a theory, in other words, a representation of reality that aspires to be accurate. We do not try to judge it, analyze it, or argue about it—these activities involve our opinionated mind. They require us to assume an attitude of a detached observer and therefore pull us away from the contemplative attitude. In text-contemplation we do not *think about* the text but *with* the text, by opening an inner clearing through which we listen to the words and resonate with them. This does not mean that we agree with what the text says—agreeing or disagreeing is not to the point at all.

Not every philosophical text is equally suitable for contemplative reading. Some texts are poetic and inspiring, while others are too wordy and intellectual; some are insightful and sensitive, while others are hackneyed or dry; some can be easily related to everyday situations, while others are abstract and remote.

It is usually best to choose a brief text of no more than three or four paragraphs in length, one that is condensed (without many repetitions or wordy explanations) and that deals with an everyday concept (self, love, freedom, etc.). Especially appropriate are philosophical texts that are written poetically. Examples are the writings of Marcus Aurelius, Nietzsche, Buber, Bergson, and Emerson, to name only a few. However, even books that are in general dry and abstract often contain moving passages, and these can be used for contemplative reading.

Contemplative exercises for individuals

Different text-contemplation exercises are suitable for different formats—group activity, counseling sessions, or individual work. Let us start with exercises that can be used by an individual or a counselee.

Silent lesson

This is a simplified, non-religious version of a traditional technique that was developed in the Middle Ages by Catholic monks of the Carthusian order, called *Lectio Divina* (divine reading). The traditional, religious procedure focuses on reading scriptures. In its philosophical form, the reading is a short philosophical text, less than a page long, preferably condensed and even poetic. The goal is to contemplate the text from a different place within us, from our inner depth, and let the text "speak" within us.

Silent lesson can be conducted by an individual, or in a counseling session between counselor and counselee, or in a group. In the individual version, if you are a single contemplator contemplating by yourself, it is best to start with a short meditative centering exercise in order to create an inner clearing. The silent lesson procedure itself is made of several steps. First, you read the selected text silently and very slowly, much slower than usual. You listen to the words of the text attentively, without imposing any opinion or analysis. Often, you will experience the text speaking within you, and ideas will appear in your mind spontaneously, by themselves so to speak. Read the same text several times.

Second, in this state of inner silence, notice a phrase or a sentence that draws your attention or "wants" to speak to you. Focus on this sentence and read it several times while listening to what it says. Various ideas may float into your mind, and when this happen, listen to them silently and try to articulate them in words. You may also write them down.

Third, after several different ideas have risen in your mind, it is time to consolidate them and give them organization and focus. To do so, gently focus your mind, notice repeating themes, and try unifying them into a single sentence that can serve as the center of all your other ideas.

Lastly, contemplate that sentence in a more relaxed fashion while taking a little walk or writing the sentence calligraphically.

In a counseling session, silent lesson is done in a similar way, but here the reading and the reflection are done mostly out loud. The counselee reads aloud the text and expresses in a few words the ideas that appear in his mind. The counselor acts as an alter ego, echoing or elaborating on the counselee's words, asking questions, and helping him articulate his ideas.

Speaking from a precious moment

This procedure is appropriate for the counseling setting. The counselee brings to his awareness a precious situation from the recent past and then tries to enter it in his mind. He imagines himself being in that past situation and tries thinking, feeling, and acting from its depth. The counselor helps him with occasional questions and comments.

The counselee's attempt to speak "from" the remembered precious moment is in effect an attempt to probe his inner depth and give voice to it. But this may not be easy, especially since it is not easy to translate a powerful experience into words. For this reason, it is usually best to do this exercise after the language of the counselee's inner dimension has been explored to some extent, and some basic concepts have been identified (see previous chapter). The counselor can use these concepts to ask relevant questions and help the counselee formulate his answers.

A guided imagined tour in a philosophical text

Guided imagery, too, can be used to reach out to the inner depth. Here the counselor chooses a short philosophical text that is similar in spirit to the counselee's inner dimension. The counselor then instructs the counselee to enter in his imagination the world of the text, and the two then explore it together.

Procedures for philosophical companionships[52]

It is sometimes difficult for counselees to contemplate in a one-on-one counseling session since they feel embarrassed and inhibited in front of the counselor's eyes. A more suitable format is the philosophical companionship. In fact, while individual counseling is an ideal format for perimeter analysis, the companionship format is ideal for experimenting with the inner dimension. The companionship enables the individual to be less self-

---

52. For a fuller and more detailed list of contemplative exercises for groups see *Handbook of Philosophical Companionships*, Vermont: Loyev Books, 2016.

absorbed and to take part in a group activity that does not revolve around him.

A sense of togetherness is very important for the success of the philosophical companionship. *Togetherness*, in its deeper sense, means that I am no longer the sole or ultimate owner of my thoughts and ideas. Like a musician in a band who resonates with his fellow players to create music together, as a companion I create with my companions the group's "music of ideas." I think primarily *with* others, rather than *about* what they say.

In ordinary groups this is not what usually happens. In a typical group discussion, for example, each individual retains his individuality and separateness and behaves like a self-sufficient, separate thinker on the topic. He has his own opinions and his own principles, and he thinks *about* the ideas of others, judging them as right or wrong. Therefore, if we want to maintain a relationship of togetherness among group members—if we want, in other words, to turn a group of people into companions who contemplate in togetherness—then certain procedures must be imposed. Such procedures might make the interaction feel "unnatural" since they pull participants out of their usual attitudes.

The topic of philosophical-contemplative companionships has been mentioned before, but we can now see more clearly how they work. A *philosophical-contemplative companionship* (or philosophical companionship for short) is a group of people who contemplate in togetherness on basic life-issues in search of meaningful philosophical insights. They meet regularly online or face-to-face, usually with a facilitator who introduces procedures and exercises. Each session is normally focused on a short philosophical text which serves as a starting point for personal-philosophical explorations.

Three general guidelines orient the activity in a companionship:

1. *Maintaining a contemplative attitude:* Companions step out of their usual opinions and thinking patterns and attempt to think and interact from a deeper aspect of

themselves. Instead of expressing automatic opinions and impersonal ideas, they give voice to their inner dimension.

2. *Resonating with others in togetherness:* Companions are no longer separate thinkers facing each other; rather, they stand side-by-side with each other, contemplating in togetherness. Instead of the usual arguing and declaring, companions resonate with each other like musicians who create together a "group-music" of understandings.

3. *Resonating with the text (or with ideas):* Companions also resonate with the philosophical text which they read together. They relate to the philosophical ideas they find in the text as one voice relates to another voice in a choir, so that agreement or disagreement is no longer to the point. The philosophical ideas in the text are not treated as a theory, in other words as a statement about the way reality really is, but as a musical sentence to resonate with, as a seed for further contemplation.

A variety of procedures and exercises can help us follow these three principles. The following are a few examples.

Voice meditation in preparation for contemplative reading
In order to make a contemplative exercise more effective, it is usually necessary to first attain an attitude of inner silence and inner listening. A brief meditative exercise of a few minutes can help create this attitude. Through this exercise we stop identifying ourselves with our busy, noisy mind and instead become a clearing, an empty space, a channel for insights to speak through us. We are no longer the self who rules and speaks and decides but are receptive and available to whatever understanding chooses to rise from our depth.

One such meditative centering exercise uses our body as a metaphor for our inner attitude. By modulating our bodily posture, we can influence our state of mind. We imagine ourselves descending along our column of air, step by step, from our nostrils through our throat and stomach to below our body. By dissociating ourselves from our head (where we usually experience ourselves to be situated), we attain a new inner attitude.

To do so, sit in a quiet place in a symmetric but comfortable position. Focus your mind on your breath as it flows in and out of your nostrils. Don't "look at" your nostrils but simply place yourself in your nostrils and rest there. If thoughts or images enter your mind, don't resist them. Ignore them and let them pass. After three slow breaths move your awareness down to your mouth, attending to the air movement; after three more slow breaths move to the entrance of your throat, then to the throat itself, to your chest, then your stomach. From there continue further down to your hips (which normally reverberate with the breathing), and finally go further down to an imaginary point underneath your chair. At this point you are no longer in your usual place in your body; you are no longer identified with your usual self. You are in what can be called, metaphorically, the point of silence, of listening, of depth.

And now, when you are "below" your usual self, "deeper" than your self, the main part of the contemplative session can begin.

Precious speaking

We distinguish between contemplative *procedures* and contemplative *exercises*. Unlike exercises, procedures are simple techniques that do not stand on their own. They can serve as elements in exercises. An exercise may contain one or more procedures.

Precious speaking is a general procedure that serves as an element in many exercises. According to this procedure, companions are instructed to speak in a concise and condensed way, as if each word is precious, as if each word is a gift to the group. They avoid repetitions, excessive explanations, and redundant words. Unnecessary words such as "Well, I think that..." are eliminated. Whenever possible, companions limit themselves to saying only one sentence at a time.

This precise way of speaking helps to pull us out of our automatic thinking and talking. It is an "unnatural" way of speaking that forces us to be intensely aware of what we are saying and how we are saying it. It also limits our ability to express a whole opinion, it focuses our minds, and it channels our thoughts and speech into a poetic mode.

Precious speaking has several versions. In *free precious speaking*, companions are invited to speak whenever they want, and they keep silence whenever they want. They may sit quietly most of the time and speak only when a sentence surfaces in their minds and "wants" to be expressed. The result is periods of silence in which participants listen inwardly, interrupted occasionally by spontaneous sentences.

Alternatively, in *rhythmic precious speaking*, companions speak in a fixed order—according to their sitting position or (in an online companionship) in alphabetical order. They are asked to speak immediately when their turn arrives, without much delay (or they may "pass" if they prefer not to speak). The result is a rhythmic sequence of pronouncements, one after the other, that resonate with each other.

Intentional conversing

Sometimes we want participants to articulate their thoughts in greater detail than permitted in the precious speaking procedure, which allows only a single, brief, condensed sentence. For example, we might want them to describe a personal experience, to reflect on the meaning of a concept or a paragraph, or to converse with each other about a given issue. At the same time, however, we don't want them to lose their contemplative state of mind and return to their usual automatic, opinionated way of thinking and conversing. The default mode of our mind is very powerful, and once we give it the opportunity, it is quick to take over.

Intentional conversing is a technique that is more relaxed than precious speaking but not completely relaxed. The contemplative attitude is maintained not by limiting speech to single sentences, but through instructions that preserve the desired inner attitude. These instructions are not really rules, since they cannot always be enforced (an inner attitude is not visible from the outside), and since they call for an inner effort. They are called "intentions."

Four intentions govern intentional conversing:

1. The intention of condensed speech: Whenever you speak, try formulating your ideas in a condensed way and avoiding repetition, excessive explanation, and unnecessary words.

2. The intention of listening: Listening to others is a crucial part of this procedure. Whenever others speak, try making their words and ideas present in your mind. To put it differently, you should open an inner space within yourself—a clearing—and place whatever is being said in this clearing. Don't agree or disagree with the speaker, don't think about how you are going to respond or what you are going to say in your turn—just make the speaker' words and ideas present in your mind.

3. The intention of speaking from the present: When you speak, give voice only to what is alive within you at the moment. Push your familiar opinions out of your mind and out of your speech, as well as any thought from the past that is no longer alive.

4. The intention of resonating: Relate to what your companions have said before you, but not by talking *about* it. Rather, *resonate with* what they have said. To do so, think of yourself as a singer in a choir. You and your companions are creating music together, each one with a different voice, improvising together as you go along. This implies that different understandings can appear side by side even if they seem to contradict each other, thus creating a polyphony of voices.

Slow reading

Slow reading is another procedure that can be used as an element in many exercises. A brief philosophical text is required for this procedure, one that is concise, rich with meaning, and not too verbose, repetitive or technical.

One of the participants starts reading the text out loud very slowly, suspending each word for a long moment. A moment of silence may be kept at the end of each sentence.

The reader might feel the automatic urge to continue to the next word, but it is important to overcome this urge and stay with the slow rhythm. The participants are instructed to listen carefully to each word, and also to the understandings that might arise within them in response. The extreme slowness of the reading, as well as the breaking of syntactic units, help break normal thinking patterns.

After the entire text has been read, the participants can share with the group their personal understandings in precious speaking, in intentional conversing, in writing, or in a drawing.

Contemplative chanting[53]

Contemplative chanting is a fourth procedure that can be incorporated in many exercises. The facilitator chooses one important sentence from the philosophical text, and the companions repeat that same sentence over and over again, one after the other, according to their sitting position (in face-to-face groups) or alphabetically (in online groups). Several rounds of re-reading of the same sentence can be done in this way. The result is an ongoing chant which gives a contemplative atmosphere and which takes the companions out of their usual thinking patterns.

Here, too, at the end of the exercise, the participants can share with the group the personal understandings that have surfaced in their minds. They can do so in precious speaking, in intentional conversing, in writing, or in a drawing.

Exercises for philosophical companionships

The above procedures are elements in larger exercises, and they are usually not independent activities that stand by themselves. The following are complete exercises that

---

53. I am indebted to my colleague Gerald Hofer who presented a powerful version of this procedure in an international online companionship which I organized in December 2015.

consist of several elements or steps. Some of them include some of the above procedures.

Silent lesson (group version)

Like the individual version described earlier, the group version of the silent lesson is a simplified version of the traditional text-contemplation called Lectio Divina. The basic idea here is that as the companions read the text in a contemplative mode, insights arise in their minds, which they then express in precious speaking. This can be followed by a second stage, in which the companions bring together those insights into a focused and coherent whole.

To begin the exercise, participants sit in a circle (or gather online), each one with a copy of the text. The text should be approximately between a paragraph and half a page in length (but it may be part of a longer text which the participants have read in advance). In order to enter a contemplative state of mind, the group starts with a short centering exercise.

In the second stage, the group reads the text together as an initial encounter with its basic ideas. This can be done in the procedure of slow reading or contemplative chanting (see above), or simply by reading the text and listening to it carefully. After each paragraph, a round of precious speaking follows in which each participant attempts to articulate in a few words the central idea which he has perceived. These words can also be written on a central sheet of paper.

While the second stage aims at achieving an initial surface understanding of the text, the next stage is fully contemplative, and it is aimed at giving voice to more personal, elaborate, creative insights. The text is read aloud either by one volunteer or each sentence by a different companion, and the reading may be repeated several times. Meanwhile, the other participants maintain receptive attention, letting the text speak within them without attempting to impose on it any analysis or explanation.

The facilitator now raises a general question about the text, such as: "What kind of love is the text trying to describe to you?" The companionship is now open for everybody to give voice to their answer in the procedure of precious speaking. The goal is to unfold a variety of insights that emerge from the original text. The emphasis at this first stage is not on organization or focus but on variety and richness.

In all the above stages, the participants should maintain a contemplative state of mind and follow the guidelines of precious speaking. This should be explained in advance.

Very often, the process so far is enough. In this case, it is time for the last step—a more relaxed round of precious speaking or intentional conversing in which the participants share what they are taking away with them from the exercise. At other times, however, an additional step is desirable, one which would allow the participants to reflect in greater detail on what has been said, and to consolidate it and bring it together into a unified whole. To do so, the participants use the intentional conversing procedure to reflect together and to formulate a sentence (or a few sentences) that would express one central understanding. They utter suggestions for such a sentence, resonating with each other and gradually converging on a single formulation.

A final round of "What am I taking away with me?" can conclude the activity.

Group poem

When we write poetically, formulating our thoughts in verse, we listen to the words in a special way. We do not look "through" the words to the idea as we usually do when we write an ordinary text, but rather attend to the words themselves, to their rhythm and sounds and shades of meaning. We therefore assume a special, intense attitude of listening which can be used for contemplation.

In this exercise, each participant receives a copy of a short condensed philosophical text. First, as in the previous exercise, the text is read out loud, and the participants briefly contemplate its surface meaning, possibly paragraph by paragraph, and comment on its straightforward meaning in precious speaking.

Once the text's basic idea is understood, it is read out loud very slowly, possibly several times. Then each participant writes a two-verse poetic piece (two lines of a poem) that expresses his personal inner response to that text.

The double verses of all the participants are then combined together on a sheet of paper, one under the other, so that they add up to one group poem. (If the group is too large, it can be divided into smaller teams, each one composing a separate poem.) Since the verses may not be congruent with each other, the group then spends some time re-ordering them and adjusting their tenses and pronouns. Every once in a while the group reads the entire poem and listens to the way it flows.

In another version of this exercise, each participant writes his own individual poem. The philosophical text is first broken into four or five parts. The first part is read slowly, and each participant resonates with it by writing the first verse of his poem. After a few minutes, the second part of the text is read, and the participants write the second line in their respective poems. A third and a fourth sentence follow until each participant has a poem made of four or five verses. The participants then take a few minutes to polish their poem and organize it. When everybody is finished, they share their poems with each other and contemplate them in togetherness.

Both versions of this exercise often yield beautiful poems that express deep understandings which surprise even the writers themselves. Evidently, the writing process is not only a way to record ideas but also to create them.

Drawing ideas

In order to express our personal understandings, we do not necessarily need to speak. Drawing sometimes enables us to give voice to what is difficult to put in words, or even escapes our awareness altogether. This is the basic idea in the exercise of drawing ideas.

As in other philosophical techniques, after a centering exercise a short philosophical text is read aloud. Then, a round of precious speaking or intentional conversing is used to make sure that everybody understands the text's surface meaning.

The text is now read slowly while participants listen quietly, inwardly. The facilitator asks the participants to draw on a sheet of paper what the text said to them personally. In order to avoid verbal thinking, they must follow the following instructions: First, do not draw anything that is an identifiable object (a flower, a face, a star, etc.). Second, do not draw any symbol that symbolizes a specific idea (for example, a red heart standing for love). Third, do not write anything on your drawing. In short, participants must draw an abstract expressionist drawing.

When the drawings are finished, they are all placed on a central table. Another blank page is placed next to each drawing. The participants walk around the table at their own free pace, looking silently at the drawings. On each blank page they write a title which they propose for the adjacent drawing (for example, "Dark clouds approaching" or "Going into myself"). When everybody has finished, each participant collects both pages and looks at the list of titles which the others have given to his drawing. This list serves as feedback that draws participants' attention to what they might not have noticed while making the drawing.

Finally, the participants sit in a circle and present to the group their drawings, as well as the feedback they had received.

Walking in a philosophical landscape

Walking in a landscape of ideas means exploring a philosophical theory from the inside, by immersing ourselves in it. We do not analyze or judge the text from the perspective of an outside observer, as we often do in academic discussions, and we do not agree or disagree with it. We place ourselves inside the reality which the text depicts and we look at what that reality is like from the perspective of somebody living in it.

As we have seen earlier in this book, a philosophical theory can be viewed as a network of ideas—a network of concepts, distinctions, assumptions, etc. It is, therefore, analogous to a landscape made of particular landmarks that are related to each other in particular ways—hills, rivers, lakes, plateaus, etc. To "walk" in this conceptual landscape is to explore the different landmarks as if they were our own reality, and to see what they mean to us when we imagine ourselves being in that world.

In a simple version of this exercise, the participants first read the text together to make sure that everybody understands its surface meaning. Then, through the procedure of precious speaking, they propose concepts which they regard as central to the text. In this way a small inventory of basic concepts is created, and the concepts are written on a central sheet of paper, spread out as a landscape of ideas. Finally, participants are asked to imagine themselves in this reality, to imagine a personal encounter with some of these concepts, and express the resulting understanding in precious speaking.

In a somewhat more complex exercise, participants are asked to think of a recent personal experience that is connected to the concepts in question. They then describe to the group that experience in the intentional conversing procedure. Others can react or ask questions about the experience.

Philosophical guided imagery

Guided imagery can be used to create a rich array of personal reactions to texts and ideas. As in the previous exercises, participants start by reading a brief philosophical text and making sure that everybody understands its surface meaning. Next, the facilitator asks them to close their eyes and imagine themselves standing in the world described in the text. Participants then explore in their imagination the landscape into which they have entered.

Obviously, a picturesque text is especially useful here. For example, the group can be instructed to imagine themselves sitting in Plato's Cave and watching the shadows on the wall. They are then instructed to imagine standing up, turning their backs to their ordinary world, walking out through the exit, and then looking at the new word they discover outside.

There are different styles of guided imagery, some of them more closely guided while others more open and free. For example, in a guided imagery of Plato's cave, the facilitator may give specific, step-by-step instructions how to leave the cave and look at the world outside. Alternatively, the facilitator may give only general guidelines at the beginning, and then let the participant leave the cave at their own individual pace and explore whatever they want.

To conclude the exercise, the participants share with each other what they have visualized and the new insights they are taking away with them.

Concluding the session

The ending of a session is an important part of the session. It is an opportunity to reflect on what has happened. Normally, the facilitator invites the participants to personally reflect on what the session had taught them, especially about themselves and ways to go beyond themselves.

Two kinds of concluding procedures should be distinguished from one another. One kind is done in the contemplative spirit, and as such it is an integral part of the session. The other kind is a free conversation, and it therefore comes after the contemplative session has ended. Both of these conclusions are important, and they can be seen as complementing each other.

In the contemplative conclusion, companions are given a few moments to reflect on the entire session, especially on the experiences and insights which they have gained during the session. Then they are asked to share what they are taking away with them, using a contemplative procedure such as precious speaking or intentional conversing.

In contrast, in the conversational conclusion the companions converse freely.

Personal variations among companions

When philosophical-contemplative exercises are conducted individually or in a one-on-one counseling setting, the selected texts and procedures can be tailored for the individual's specific orientation. Depending on the individual's personal perimeter and the apparent language of his inner depth, appropriate texts and procedures can be selected that are related to his perimeter, yearnings, overall dissatisfactions, and precious moments.

In a companionship, however, it is difficult to deal with each participant's specific perimeter and inner depth. Philosophical contemplation in groups deals primarily with general life-issues and with texts that are selected for the entire group. A philosophical-contemplative exercise on a text by Plato, for example, does not necessarily relate directly to Sarah's yearning to overcome her sense of emptiness towards a sense of plenitude, or with David's yearning to overcome his isolation towards a sense of togetherness with the world.

Even so, philosophical-contemplative exercises are still helpful to most participants because they give each one enough freedom to relate to the ideas and experiences that are personally relevant. Philosophical texts deal with basic life-issues, and a life-issue by its very nature projects on many aspects of life. When participants are asked to select a personal experience or focus on a sentence that speaks to them, they naturally choose what touches them personally. This is especially the case with participants who are already familiar with their perimeter and with some aspects of the landscape outside it.

For the facilitator, it is therefore important to construct the exercises in a way that would give participants the personal freedom to select which words, ideas, or experiences they wish to focus on. For example, instructing companions to choose for contemplation a sentence that attracts their attention is better than asking all of them to contemplate the same sentence.

Case study: a philosophical companionship

Linda organizes a weekend retreat for a new philosophical companionship. The eleven companions meet on Friday afternoon in a quiet house in the country, where they are to spend their time in philosophical contemplation until Sunday night.

On Friday afternoon, they gather and briefly introduce themselves to each other. For the first session, on Friday evening, Linda has chosen the topic of sources of the self. "Not everything we say or feel or think comes from the same place within us," Linda explains her choice to the group. "Many of our thoughts, for example, come from a superficial, automatic level of thinking—they come and go without much reflection. But at other times, a new understanding may stir up something deep in us. Does this make sense to you?"

"Sure," Melanie says. "Sometimes a sentence I read in a book strikes me, and I feel it is telling me something important. I need to stop reading and think."

Jonathan nods. "Or, a sentence in a song can hit me, I'm not even sure why. I feel there is something deep in it, you know what I mean? The rest of the song may be just ordinary, but this particular sentence touches something deep in me."

A few others share similar experiences.

"Nice," Linda agrees. "Of course, 'deep' is a metaphor. We are hoping this weekend to have experiences and understandings that could be described as 'deep,' so we'd better start by reflecting on the meaning of this metaphor."

A couple of participants want to express their opinions, but Linda gently stops them. "Let's not start our exploration with opinions. Opinions are too easy to invent and declare. What, after all, can opinions tell us about an issue that is beyond opinions? Let's try to contemplate on the issue."

Linda now hands out a short text by the 19th-century American philosopher Ralph Waldo Emerson. "Emerson talks in this poetic piece about what he calls 'the over-soul'—the higher source of our inspiration and creativity, which is close enough to what we call 'depth.' But we don't need to agree or disagree with him. For us, this text is not a theory that is correct or incorrect, but a starting point for contemplation that can trigger our thoughts. It is like a musical phrase that can inspire us to compose our personal music of ideas."

The rest of the session consists of two main stages. The first stage is devoted to an initial examination of the three short paragraphs which Linda has chosen, although not in an objective and detached manner but in a personal and contemplative way. After a brief meditative centering exercise, the companions open their eyes and look at the text in their hands. They read together the first sentence— each companion reads it out loud slowly, one after the other according to their sitting order, repeating it again and again. When all have read the first sentence, they continue to the second sentence, and then to the third. The many repetitions of the same words give the participants a strange sense of disorientation. They are no longer thinking in their familiar, automatic way. As the words are being repeated, images and thoughts start hovering in their minds.

"Man is a stream whose source is hidden. Our being descends into us from we know not from where. The most exact calculator cannot predict that something incalculable may not happen the very next moment. I am forced every moment to acknowledge a higher origin of events than the will I call 'mine'..."[54]

Linda signals to the group to stop reading. It is time to contemplate what they have read so far. Using the free precious speaking procedure, they each say in one sentence what they find central or significant in this paragraph.

"I do not fully belong to myself," says Larry, "and my thoughts and actions do not fully belong to me."

---

54. "The Over-soul," in William Gilman (ed.), *Selected Writings of Ralph Waldo Emerson*, New York: New American Library, 1965, p. 281.

After a short silence, Tammy offers, "I am not completely one—part of me comes from myself, part of me comes from elsewhere."

Another silence follows. This time it is interrupted by Sally, who paraphrases Emerson's sentence. "I am a stream whose source is hidden."

"I don't fully know myself," Becca says after a long silence, "because I don't fully know what may touch me five minutes from now."

After all the participants have spoken, Linda invites responses that would integrate together what everybody has said into one unifying theme. "Try speaking now not for yourself but for the entire group. Try giving voice to the many sentences we have just heard."

"I am more than my familiar self," Tammy says.

"I am much more than my familiar self," Larry repeats.

Three more similar sentences are voiced, and it is clear that the group agrees on a common central theme in the first paragraphs. Overall, the contemplation on the first paragraph has taken a little more than ten minutes. Linda now invites them to move on to the second paragraph. Again the participants read the paragraph sentence by sentence, repeating each sentence many times, and then giving voice to their understanding in precious speaking.

At the end of about forty minutes, after they have finished with the three paragraphs, Linda moves on to a more personal exercise.

"Now that we have a personal understanding of each paragraph, let us look at the text as a whole—but in a more personal way. What do you personally hear the text telling you? What is it calling you to see or do? I am not asking you what it tells you about human beings in general, but what it says to you. Take a few moments to reflect on this."

She waits a few moments, then adds, "But let's not think about it in an abstract way. Please read the text silently to yourself, very slowly over and over again, and let the answer come up within you. Notice a word or phrase that touches you, that attracts your attention, that 'calls you.' Listen quietly to what it tells you—and write it down for yourself. Then share with us whatever you feel comfortable sharing."

When everybody has finished writing, the companions put down their pens and start a round of sharing. This time the procedure is no longer in precious speaking, because Linda wants the participants to speak a little more freely and in greater detail. She therefore proposes a procedure of intentional conversing. As mentioned earlier, here the emphasis is not on what you have to say but on a special kind of listening: You push aside your thoughts and opinions and open a "clearing"—an inner space of silence and listening. When others speak, you place their words in your clearing.

Linda asks the companions to start by explaining which sentence or phrase in the text touched them.

"I was struck by the words 'our being descends into us,'" Rick starts. "They showed me that I should remember my 'higher' being and that I should let it descend into me. I am here on earth, always busy, always doing a million things, and the sentence told me: Stop, Rick, stop! Take a break every once in a while and just be quiet."

For lack of time, Linda decides not to invite others to ask Rick questions about his insight. Anne then describes her own insight, and a few others follow her for some ten minutes.

"Thank you all for sharing," Linda says. "Before we continue, let us go back to the text so that we remain connected to it. It is the central axis of our session tonight."

The group goes back to Emerson. In the spirit of contemplation which has been developing for a while in the room, they read him slowly and repeatedly so that the overall effect is that of chanting.

"And now," Linda says, "we are ready for our last exercise. Let's try to connect our Emersonian insights to actual experiences we have experienced. Please take a few moments and think about a specific experience you recently had that resembles your understanding of Emerson's words."

Linda lets the companions reflect silently for a few moments. "Everybody found a recent Emersonian experience? Good. Now, let's write it down and then share it with each other. However, we don't need to hear about the details of you experience—how exactly it happened, where and when. We only want to hear the essence. So please give voice to your over-soul experience in a poetic way. In other words, please write two poetic verses that give voice to your experience."

"Wait a minute, Linda," Debbie interrupts. "Do you mean a poetic description of the feeling I had?"

Linda shakes her head with a smile. "No more instructions. You are free to write any two verses that come to your mind and that give voice to your experience."

After a few minutes, when the writing ends, the companions copy their verses on a large sheet of paper, one under the other, so they add up to one long poem. A volunteer reads the poem out loud, and then a second volunteer and a third.

I was wrapped in blankets of shyness and inhibitions,
But then an animating spirit came and blew them away.

A single word is sometimes sufficient
to trigger a river of unknown energies.

I had no words to utter, my mind was tired and blank.
Yet something in me demanded to speak, and I let it do
so.

I know it is me, and I know it's not me,
as small as I am, and as big as the world.

(And so on...)

The emerging poem is not yet finished. Some adjustments are needed to make it flow coherently, and the group works on it for a while. The final group-poem is read slowly, while the participants listen silently.

"By way of concluding our contemplation today," Linda says, "let us take a few moments to reflect on what has happened to us in this session. Ask yourself: What did the ideas we have encountered help me see or understand?"

Sarah is the first to speak. "Emerson made me wonder if I'm not too self-controlled. Shouldn't I be more silent and receptive to what life is telling me?"

"What was powerful to me," says Rick, "was not so much the ideas themselves but the sense of listening to them in profound silence. It was wondrous to hear them floating into my mind and then floating away and disappearing. That made me understand that my ideas are not always in my control. I don't know if I believe in Emerson's over-soul, but I definitely have a fountain of ideas. That's something new to me."

"I had a similar experience," Debbie replies. "I felt that I was letting something inside me speak, especially in the precious speaking rounds at the beginning. I should try to give more space to that 'something.'"

"Your over-soul," Michael mumbles.

"I don't want to give it a title. Over-soul, my hidden self, the inner depth—the name doesn't matter. The point is that some part of me that is usually quiet started speaking."

Others, too, had similar experiences.

"It seems, then," Linda summarizes, "that in this session we gave voice to something within us that we don't usually pay attention to. And when we give it voice, we are awakening it, we are cultivating it. Cultivating our inner dimension or inner depth is a long process. But in this retreat we will start working on it."

Linda's companionship session illustrates how contemplative exercises can help companions activate a dormant dimension within themselves. This is, in effect, an important step in the process of stepping out of our Platonic cave. As we have seen, our Platonic cave is our "perimeter"—our rigid and automatic conception of life, which we express through our normal patterns of thought, emotions, and behavior. Philosophical self-reflection and contemplation can help us recognize them, step out of them, and develop a broader attitude to ourselves and our world, an attitude that involves more of ourselves, especially the inner dimension of our being.

Maintaining the contemplative attitude throughout the day

The exercises presented above are, no doubt, only the beginning of a longer process. It is not easy to maintain a contemplative attitude throughout the day and to push aside our automatic self. Our daily errands, pressures, and conversations keep diverting our attention and pulling us back to our ordinary perimetral attitudes. Even after a powerful contemplative exercise, we tend to forget all about it and quickly lose ourselves in our daily matters. It is therefore important to persist in contemplative-philosophical exercises in order to achieve a meaningful self-transformation.

Here are several suggestions about how to do it:

- Start the day with a session of about ten minutes (or more) of contemplative reading.

- During the rest of the day, try to maintain in your mind a selected sentence from the text you have read, as well as the understandings that surfaced within you while contemplating on it. Don't analyze them, but simply make them present in your mind. Let them speak if they "wish" to speak, and follow them wherever they take you. It is possible that by the end of the day those understandings will take you far away from where you started in the morning.

- If you are like most normal people, you will probably lose your contemplative attitude many times during the day for long periods of time. This is normal and no reason for distress. But it is recommended that you periodically practice a brief *recollection exercise* in order to bring yourself back to the contemplative mode. One such exercise consists of making a small pre-selected gesture that serves as a reminder. For example, whenever you recall your morning contemplation and realize that you have lost it, touch gently the center of your forehead or chest and gather yourself back into yourself.

- Another recollection exercise is *presencing*, in other words making something present in your awareness. Several times during the day try to "presence" whatever is happening to you at the moment: your bodily motions, your thoughts, feelings, reactions, as well as people and things around you. While presencing, don't judge and analyze and don't look at yourself from the outside, from the perspective of an external observer. Simply let the presenced object be present intensely in your awareness. You can practice this presencing exercise for a minute or two at a time, or possibly longer, while you are waiting for a bus, or eating, or walking, or even conversing. It can serve to bring you back to the contemplative attitude.

Such a contemplative schedule, even if you lose it during most of the day (as you probably will), is likely to open you to new understandings. Some of them will probably arise from the text you have read in the morning.

You will soon learn that not only new understandings but also the contemplative openness itself—the clearing— are to some extent like unexpected "gifts." They do not fully depend on our own efforts. Sometimes they refuse to arrive no matter how eagerly we invite them. At other times they pervade us as if by themselves, without effort, for no apparent reason. In those special moments, we may experience ourselves as part of a greater realm of life and reality.

Nevertheless, as mentioned earlier, to some extent clearings do depend on our efforts and attention. They are in part the fruit of work and experience. By working consistently on our contemplation, we can gradually learn to develop a steadier and deeper contemplative attitude. We can then learn how to be involved in our daily errands while at the same time also be present beyond our perimeter.

Chapter 11

Polyphonic Wisdom and Beyond

We began our philosophical journey with the observation that much of our normal life is limited to narrow, rigid, automatic patterns of thought, emotion, and behavior. This insight has been expressed by many important thinkers throughout the ages. It is also witnessed by our own yearning to live life more fully and meaningfully. I called these boundaries our "perimeter," or, using Plato's image, our "cave."

Those thinkers whom I called "transformational philosophers" have made profound observations about the way to step beyond our small lives. Each of them, however, expressed only one specific way of understanding our perimeter and transcending it, a way that is often too limited and dogmatic. As I suggested, if we want to go beyond the narrowness and dogmatism of any specific philosophical theory, we must realize that life is more complex and multifaceted than any single theory. People are different, their perimeters are different, and the potential ways to step beyond their boundaries are different.

On the basis of years of working with individuals and with groups, I proposed in this book a more pluralistic approach that accepts personal and philosophical variations. Rather than imposing on life a ready-made theory, we should respect the many voices of life. We should listen to the way the individual's life speaks, learn its unique perimeter, its specific concepts and language, and the unique way to transcend it.

In the first stage of our journey, we investigated the landscape of our perimeter. We then explored the second step in the philosophical process, namely the stepping beyond the perimeter. Both of these stages were based on the power of ideas, or the power of understanding. Philosophical ideas have tremendous richness and depth, and as such they can enlighten us about the foundation of our prison, as well as about possible ways to step beyond it. They can also inspire us to take this step out.

The problem is that our own ideas are usually limited. If you ask ordinary people about the nature of love or of freedom, for example, there is usually little they can say beyond simplistic formulas or popular slogans. Fortunately, the history of philosophy contains many treasures of wisdom. Numerous thinkers throughout the ages have explored basic life-issues and have written a wide variety of deep texts about them. Reflecting on historical philosophical texts can, therefore, enrich our exploration and help us develop our personal understanding of our perimeter and of what lies beyond it.

Philosophical ideas as voices of reality

When we learn to listen to philosophical ideas from the depth of our being—not just from our analytic thought, not just from our opinions—then an amazing thing happens. We then find ourselves in an altogether new state of mind, one that is not bound by superficial and automatic thinking patterns. This is a state of special openness to the complex fabric of human reality. We no longer feel a need to agree or disagree with this or that philosophical text, because those texts are no longer theories about human reality. They are some of the many voices with which life speaks in us, and as such they can touch us, inspire us, resonate within us.

We then realize that life also speaks in philosophical writings—after all, they have been written by human beings like you and me—and through them it speaks within us and give birth to our own understandings and insights. Life, or more generally human reality, is no longer an array of objective facts that stand out there in front of the objective gaze of an uninvolved spectator. Understanding reality is no longer limited to opinions or theories about this or that fact. Human reality, rather than being a factual spectacle, resonates within us. It has raised in the minds of great thinkers profound understandings, and when we read their writings it now generates new understandings within us too. Although life speaks in its many voices through all of us, great thinkers have the ability to articulate these voices in inspiring ways.

The ability to listen to the voices of human reality depends on our ability to step out of the cave of our normal, superficial, rigid attitudes, in other words out of our perimeter. Once we have taken a step out of our perimetral attitudes, even if for a few minutes, we can understand basic life-issues in fundamentally new ways. We can then hear the voices of life rising within us and inspiring new insights. These are no longer our personal opinions that we produce with our personal smartness. They are expressions of human life as it resonates within us. When we read a deep philosophical text, its words are not a theory *about* reality, but an understanding that comes to us *from* reality. Its secret power does not lie in its theoretical accuracy or in its capacity to "capture" the facts with its statements. No single theory can do that. Their secret lies in their capacity to resonate within us and inspire us to give voice to life.

From this perspective, a deep philosophy should not be viewed as a theory—as a system that aspires to be an accurate picture of the world, even if the writer intended it to be this way. This is not why it touches us. If we want a philosophical text to elevate us, if we want it to expand us beyond our rigid perimetral attitudes, then we should treat it as a voice that speaks to us and speaks in us, one which calls us to resonate with it and express life as it speaks in us.

Life speaks in us in a polyphonic choir. We can develop an awareness of this polyphony—or what can be called *polyphonic awareness*—if we manage to step out of our narrow perimeter and listen to the voices of wisdom from our inner dimension, from our inner depth. In this sense, contemplating on philosophical ideas means listening to the polyphony of human reality as it resonates within us. And this new polyphonic awareness, which comes from our inner dimension, also serves to give voice to that inner dimension, awaken it, and cultivate it within us. This is, then, the main goal of our philosophical journey, described by the many transformational philosophers throughout the ages: stepping out of our perimeter towards a fullness of being which can be appreciated from our inner depth.

Clearly, stepping beyond our perimeter in this sense does not mean getting rid of all our behavioral or emotional patterns. As human beings flesh and blood with biological and psychological makeup, we cannot become angels. A tree cannot shed away the biological structures that make it a tree; in fact, it *needs* these structures.

Nevertheless, we can stop limiting ourselves to these structures and become more than them. Our perimeter is part of us, but it is not all there is to us. By analogy, our skeleton is an essential part of us, but we are more than our skeleton. Likewise, we cannot and should not get rid of the pain mechanism in our body, our hunger mechanism, or our fear mechanism, but we need not be imprisoned in them and controlled by them. We are more than these functions. We can be aware of our headache or our fear and yet not be prisoners of these automatic feelings. In this sense, we can rise above them.

Stepping beyond our perimeter and being open to the voices of wisdom may be impossible to do all the time. Occasionally we will find our behavior and emotions hijacked by our old perimeter just as before. But side by side with this automatic perimeter, we will also have the broader polyphonic awareness that involves our inner depth. Our old behavioral and emotional patterns will not disappear, although they will most likely be weakened. Much of ourselves—our behavior, emotions, thoughts— will still remain within the old boundaries of our usual perimeter. Nevertheless, we will no longer be totally immersed in them and controlled by them. A new dimension of our being will gradually appear, expressed as a new awareness that is not limited to any specific theory or attitude. We will now have an awareness that overlooks all attitudes, that appreciates the voices of reality as a whole without identifying ourselves with any particular one.

This new openness to the many voices of reality is a form of wisdom. It is the capacity to rise above our private theory and be part of a larger horizon of life, to belong not just to this or that approach but to the entire symphony of voices that speak in life.

Conclusion: Towards an uncharted terrain

What I am saying here is no doubt vague. One would want to know more about the precise nature of polyphonic awareness, about the inner dimension or depth, and about the landscape beyond the perimeter.

However, our discussion of the philosophical-contemplative process must end here, even though the process itself should go on. Because at this point we are entering an uncharted terrain. From this point on, instructions can only impede. True going-beyond must transcend all instructions and methods, all that is pre-determined and generalized, away from roads that have been paved in advance. Only so can the exploration become truly philosophical, personal, and open to new horizons. It may lead to unexpected regions, and it may even end up contradicting things that have been said in previous stages of the journey, as helpful as they had been back then. Here Wittgenstein's dictum is most appropriate, that once we have climbed the ladder we should kick it away.[55]

There is a great temptation to set down rules and impose general theories. This is witnessed vividly in the history of religions. Even in matters of divine reality and mystical experiences which are generally ineffable and beyond human concepts, thinkers throughout the ages kept building doctrines and alleged "truths." This is a temptation we ought to resist. We must let go of doctrines.

---

55. Ludwig Wittgenstein, *Tractatus Logico-Philosophicus*, New York: Routledge, 1974, section 6.54.

We started this book with the first steps of the philosophical journey. In these early stages, the issues were still subject to analysis and generalization because they dealt with perimeters. Perimeters are structured by their very nature, and to a considerable extent their landscape can be charted. The more we continued towards the process of stepping out of the cave and exploring that which lies outside it, the less there was to say in a precise and general way. To be sure, even in those later chapters of the book I suggested various guidelines, methods, and exercises. But they were intended to serve as seeds for personal experimentation, as tentative signposts to be transcended. And now, even those tentative signposts must be left behind as we head towards a path that is essentially personal and awaiting discovery. As Nietzsche's Zarathustra says: "Now I go alone, my disciples. You too go now, alone. Thus I want it. Verily, I counsel you: Go away from me and resist Zarathustra! ... One repays a teacher badly if one always remains nothing but a pupil."[56]

---

56. Friedrich Nietzsche, *Thus Spoke Zarathustra*, part 1, "The Gift-Giving Virtue," section 3. In Walter Kaufmann (ed.), *The Portable Nietzsche*, New York: Viking Penguin, 1982, p. 190.

Lightning Source UK Ltd.
Milton Keynes UK
UKOW05f1013030417
298197UK00001B/271/P